The Vision of Nietzsche

Philip Novak is Professor and Chairman of the Department of Philosophy and Religion at Dominican College in San Rafael, California, where he has taught courses in the world's religions, the philosophy and psychology of religion, the history of philosophy, and social ethics since 1980. He is the author of *The World's Wisdom* and *Religion and Altruism* and has written numerous articles in professional and popular journals.

The Spirit of Philosophy Series

"This series of books offers the core teachings of the world's greatest philosophers, considered for the light their writings throw on the moral and material crises of our time. Repositioned in this way, philosophy and the great philosophers may once again serve humankind's eternal and ever-new need to understand who we are, why we are here, and how we are to live."

Jacob Needleman, Ph.D.
Series Editor

In the same series

THE SPIRIT OF PHILOSOPHY SERIES

The Vision of Nietzsche

Introduced and edited by
Philip Novak

Man's last and highest parting is when, for
God's sake, he takes leave of God.
— MEISTER ECKHART

To Bridgett

A catalogue record for this book is available from the British Library.

ISBN 1-84333-352-X
Printed by CPD Wales, Ebbw Vale
Cover design by Andrew Sutterby

© Vega 2001

Published in 2001 by
Vega
64 Brewery Road
London N7 9NY

Visit our website at
www.chrysalisbooks.co.uk

CONTENTS

Key to Title Initials

A   *The Anti-Christ*. Written in September 1888, published in 1895.

AOM   *Assorted Opinions and Maxims*. Published in 1879 as the First Supplement to *Human, All Too Human*; 2nd edition published in 1886.

BGE   *Beyond Good and Evil*. Published in 1886.

D   *Daybreak*. Published in 1881; 2nd edition published in 1886.

EH   *Ecce Homo*. Written in the autumn of 1888, published in 1908.

GM   *On the Genealogy of Morals*. Published in 1887.

GS   *The Gay Science*. Published in 1882; 2nd, expanded edition published in 1887.

HA   *Human, All Too Human*. Published in 1878; 2nd edition published in 1886.

T   *Twilight of the Idols*. Written in the summer of 1888, published in 1889.

WS   *The Wanderer and his Shadow*. Published in 1880 as the Second Supplement to *Human, All Too Human*; 2nd edition published in 1886.

Z   *Thus Spoke Zarathustra*. Parts I and II published in 1883, Part III published in 1884, Part IV written in 1885, published in 1892.

The alphanumerics after the title initials at the foot of each extract refer to the section of the book from which the extract is taken.

Chronological Order of The Above Works

HA (1878), HA Preface (1886)
AOM (1879)
WS (1880)
D (1881)
GS (1882), GS expanded (1887)
Z (1883–85)
BGE (1886)
GM (1887)
T (1888)
A (1888)
EH (1888)

Notes on the Text

Following Nietzsche's customary practice, we have num-
bered each selection in the book. The original source for
each selection is referenced directly beneath it in brackets.

Selections in each chapter are arranged in chronological
order.

Bracketed ellipses [. . .] belong to the editor and indicate
elided text. Unbracketed ellipses are Nietzsche's own.

Acknowledgements

Acknowlegement is made that copyright material from the following books is reproduced by permission of Penguin Books Ltd: TWILIGHT OF THE IDOLS, OR, HOW TO PHILOSOPHIZE WITH A HAMMER; THE ANTI-CHRIST by Friedrich Nietzsche, translated by R.J. Hollingdale (Penguin Classics, 1968), translation copyright © R.J. Hollingdale; BEYOND GOOD AND EVIL by Friedrich Nietzsche, translated by R.J. Hollingdale (Penguin Classics, 1973, revised edition 1990), translation copyright © R.J. Hollingdale, 1973, 1990; A NIETZSCHE READER translated by R.J. Hollingdale (Penguin Classics, 1977), translation copyright © R.J. Hollingdale, 1977; THUS SPOKE ZARATHUSTRA by Friedrich Nietzsche, translated by © R.J. Hollingdale (Penguin Classics, 1961), copyright © R.J. Hollingdale, 1961, 1969; ECCO HOMO by Friedrich Nietzsche, translated by © R.J. Hollingdale (Penguin Classics, 1979), translation copyright © R.J. Hollingdale, 1979.

Acknowledgement is made to Penguin US for the use of material from the following: THE PORTABLE NIETZSCHE by Friedrich Nietzsche, selected and translated, with an introduction, prefaces, and notes, by Walter Kaufmann, (New York: Viking Press, 1954).

Acknowledgement is made to Cambridge University Press for permission to use material from the following: DAYBREAK, by Friedrich Nietzsche, Cambridge University Press, 1982; HUMAN, ALL TOO HUMAN, by Friedrich Nietzsche, Cambridge University Press, 1986.

Acknowledgement is made for the use of material from the following: ON THE GENEALOGY OF MORALS, translated by Walter Kaufmann and R.J. Hollingale, copyright © 1967 by Random House, Inc., reprinted by permission of Random House, Inc.; THE GAY SCIENCE, translated, with commentary, by Walter Kaufmann, copyright © 1974 by Random House, Inc., reprinted by permission of Random House, Inc.

The author has made every effort to trace the copyright holders of the extracts in this book. If he has inadvertently overlooked any, he will be pleased to make the necessary arrangements at the first opportunity.

PART ONE
General Introduction

Life and Work

Nietzsche was born in Röcken, Germany, on 15 October 1844, and was raised in an atmosphere of pious Lutheran Christianity. His literary proclivities surfaced early. At 14 he was already critically appraising the output of his earlier years and producing home-made books of new poems and essays.

From 1858 (age 14) to 1864, he attended the elite Pforta school where he received a first-rate classical education. In 1864 at the University of Bonn, he began to study theology, but a growing skepticism, abetted by his discovery of the writings of Schopenhauer, put an end to this. He switched to the study of classical philology first at Bonn, then at the University of Leipzig. By the age of 23 he had gained so great a reputation that he was appointed Professor of Classical Philology at the University of Basel, Switzerland, before having attained his doctorate, which was later awarded to him without examination. One of his awestruck professors spoke for many when in a letter of recommendation he described the brilliant young Nietzsche as a "phenomenon."

Nietzsche taught at Basel for ten years (1869–79), but was never satisfied with the "mole-like activities" of university scholars and "their indifference to the urgent

problems of life."[1] Though named a full professor in
1870, Nietzsche already knew that the regime of the university was incompatible with the unfettered thinking he
felt called to do.

In 1876, Nietzsche took a year-long sick leave from
the university and began writing *Human, All Too
Human*. He later explained the significance of the title:
"where *you* see ideal things, *I* see—human, alas all too
human things!"[2] No words could better express the skeptical and nihilistic tendencies that were to dominate
Nietzsche's thought from this point forward. Deeply
influenced by Darwin's vision of humanity as an outgrowth of the natural and animal worlds, Nietzsche sus-
pected that the human intellect and its spiritual
products—culture, morality, religion—are ultimately gov-
erned by biological imperatives. Religious beliefs, far
from forming a true picture of some higher world, are
self-deceptions that feed on visceral fears and cravings.
God, truth, free will—the very foundations of our self-
assessment as higher creatures—are fictions. We are
clever animals but our cleverness is meaningless, for
there is no overarching purpose to life, no larger story in
which we play a role. Humanity stands alone, projecting
its futile metaphysical dreams upon a dark and indifferent infinity of space.

Human, All Too Human appeared in 1878 and sold
a meager 170 copies in its first year. Yet Nietzsche now
took permanent leave of the university and, supported
only a by a modest pension, began to wander, seasonal-
ly, from place to place in Switzerland, southern France,
northern Italy and Germany. The solitary nomad would
rent a spartan, poorly heated room (the only sort he
could afford), take a daily walk in the surrounding
heights, and then return to write the books he knew

would change the world. This was to be the basic pattern of his life for the next ten years. It was to be a decade of maddening, nearly unendurable loneliness, exacerbated by severely deteriorating health. The myopia he had inherited from his father had now rendered him nearly blind. Excruciating migraines that had plagued him since pre-adolescence now tortured him for hours and sometimes days at a time. Painful cramps regularly clawed at his sensitive stomach, often resulting in fits of spasmodic vomiting that lasted for days on end. Chronic insomnia singed his nerves until he drugged himself to sleep with chloral hydrate.

And yet, under such conditions this desperately ill and lonely man would produce at least one new book for every year of that decade, books written in such a vivid and electrifying style that in twenty-five hundred years the only world-class philosopher who stands in the same rank of literary genius is Plato.

In quick succession came *Assorted Opinions and Maxims* (1879), *The Wanderer and his Shadow* (1880), *Daybreak* (1881), *The Gay Science* (1882), *Thus Spoke Zarathustra* (1883–85), *Beyond Good and Evil* (1886), *On the Genealogy of Morals* (1887), and in 1888, the final year of his creative life, *Twilight of the Idols*, *The Anti-Christ*, and *Ecce Homo*.

Up until 1881, Nietzsche wrote almost exclusively in the skeptical, destructive vein he gleefully called "philosophy with a hammer." But in August of 1881, Nietzsche wrote to a friend: "Ideas have arisen on my horizon the likes of which I have never seen before [. . .] I [am . . .] filled with a new vision." A few months later, Nietzsche proclaimed that he was finished with negation: "I want to be at all times hereafter only an affirmer [*ein Ja-sagender*]!³ Nietzsche had found God unbelievable, but he had also found nihilism unlivable. To be sure, Nietzsche never really abandoned his critical stance—it was with him, dominantly, to the end. But from this time on Nietzsche sought to create in its very midst a new redemptive vision for a world in which the old God had died. It would revolve around the figure of the superman and his life-afffirming, earth-embracing, despair-defying, joyful wisdom—recurrent themes in *Zarathustra* and later writings.

In the first days of the new year, 1889, Nietzsche suffered a total mental collapse. His paralyzed body and the remains of his mind lived on until August 1900, but he wrote nothing more. The cause of Nietzsche's insanity has never been satisfactorily determined. It is often attributed to the spread of a syphilitic infection he contracted in his student days, but this hypothesis does not perfectly fit the facts. According to one of his recent biographers, we cannot fully dismiss the possibility that non-organic factors were involved.[4]

Here is R.J. Hollingdale's poignant comment on Nietzsche's last years:

> . . . his [. . .] books fell dead from the press [. . .]. Until the end of 1887, in spite of having produced a series of books without equal in the German literature of their time and now world-famous, he was virtually unknown. [. . .] It was not until the 1890s that [. . .] his reputation suddenly soared, so that by 1900 he was famous, not to say notorious. Of this he knew nothing, having become mentally a child again. Alone, ill and unsuccessful, Nietzsche in the 1880s is however not a figure to pity: in one book after another, couched in a style it must have been a

perpetual delight to realize, he celebrated as no one else has ever done the splendour, power and joy of life.[5]

---

[1] Letter to Erwin Rohde, 20 November 1868. Cited in J.P. Stern, *Friedrich Nietzsche*, New York, Penguin, 1979, 34.

[2] Friedrich Nietzsche, *Ecce Homo*, translated with an introduction by R.J. Hollingdale, New York, Penguin, 1979, 89.

[3] GS 276.

[4] Hayman, Ronald, *Nietzsche: A Critical Life*, Oxford University Press, New York, 1989, 10–11.

[5] Friedrich Nietzsche, *Twilight of the Idols* and *The Anti-Christ*, translated with an introduction and commentary by R.J. Hollingdale, New York, Penguin, 1968, 14.

A Review of the Chapters and Nietzsche's Central Ideas

Prior to his mental breakdown, Nietzsche had been planning a book to crown and complete his work. Its planned title was *The Will to Power: A Revaluation of All Values*. And that, with characteristic Nietzschean economy, says it all. Once one begins to understand life in terms of the will to power, everything shifts. Everything human beings hitherto valued *must* now be re-valued in the light of this new understanding. The results of Nietzsche's revaluation are the subjects of "The Destroyer" and "The Creator". In "The Fulcrum", however, the focus is the will to power itself, the gateway to Nietzsche's thought.

The Will to Power

What, then, is the will to power? It is life's intrinsic and inexorable ache for *more*. Living processes incessantly seek the enjoyment of their own sensorium, the unblocked expression of their vitality, the radiance of their health, the venting of their strength, the overcoming of resistances, and the amplification of their self-feeling. Life in each and every one of its infinite manifestations carries within it a will to fulfillment, a will to expansion, a will to deeper, fuller being. Many words are possible and perhaps necessary to describe this indescribable tropism at the heart of life, but Nietzsche chose the German *macht*—power. The will to power, Nietzsche tells us, includes but exceeds the will to self-preservation. For it seeks not only the continuance of life, but *more* life, an *intensification* of life. "Energy is eternal delight" says the poet William Blake, and these words draw us directly into the Nietzschean atmosphere. Hidden in the coils of our intestines, the throb of our blood and the biochemistries of our brains, the will to power is the great motivator behind the immense variety of human activity. It is the single music behind and within the multiform dance of life. In Nietzsche's more technical language:

> Granted finally that one succeeded in explaining our entire instinctual life as the development and ramification of one basic form of will—as will to power, as is *my* theory—; granted that one could trace all organic functions back to this will to power and could also find in it the solution to the problem of procreation and nourishment—they are *one* problem—one would have acquired the right to define *all* efficient force unequivocally as: *will to power*. The world seen from within, the world described and defined according to its "intelligible character"—it would be "will to power" and nothing else.

Insight into the will to power means that we may never forget that humanity's roots lie in the organic and animal worlds. Yet Nietzsche also saw that only the *human* animal can *transmute* the will to power so as to evolve toward a new, more-than-animal condition. Nietzsche's thought constantly moves between his disgust at the current state of humankind and his hope for a higher, transformed humanity. The bridge between them is a sublimated will to power. Relatively crude manifestations of the will to power such as power *over* (others) can give way to subtler expressions, as in power over oneself (self-discipline) and, especially, power *for* creation. Nietzsche hints at the spectrum of refinement to which the will to power is subject in calling philosophy's quest for truth "the most spiritual will to power." [BGE 9]

Truth

"The Labyrinth of Truth" draws us into Nietzsche's complex relationship to truth. While still a young man, Nietzsche wrote a letter to his sister in which he renounces the comforts of religious faith in order to freely pursue objective truth. As the course of his life makes abundantly clear, he never wavered from this vocation. He valued nothing higher than the attainment of truth and, like an ascetic bent on God, abandoned almost everything that belonged to a normal worldly life in order to pursue it.

Yet, in the midst of this powerful truth-search, there runs an equally powerful countercurrent of skepticism. Nietzsche harbors a suspicion that the real truth about "objective truth" is that the latter is a fiction. Every candidate for 'truth' must first be expressed in language, and language, Nietzsche reminds us, is notoriously unable to get at reality. It oversimplifies and distorts, concealing at least as much as it reveals. Words, like a hall of mirrors, reflect only each other and in the end point back to the conditions of their users, without having established anything about the way things really are.

Nietzsche's skepticism about truth is also a consequence of his insight into the will to power. "Will to power" means that our mental life is secretly directed by our instinctual drives. Concepts are little more than puppets at the ends of strings pulled by organismic needs. Even our so-called will to truth is a mask worn by the will to power. "Truth" is the name we give to that which agrees with our instinctual preferences; it is what we call our *interpretation* of the world, especially when we want to foist it on others. There are no eternal facts, says Nietzsche, there are only interpretations, orchestrated by the will to power.

If we wish to turn this dictate on Nietzsche himself, we would find that he has already beaten us to the punch: "Granted this too is only interpretation—and you will be eager enought to raise this objection?—well, so much the better." [BGE 22] But can Nietzsche really mean it? Did he believe that the will to power, for example, was itself only an interpretation, valid for him but not necessarily for anyone else and no truer than any other interpretation of reality? Surely not. Nietzsche was trapped. On the one hand, he saw that given the infirmities of language and the imperatives of our biology, "truth" was a will-o'-the-wisp, a human pretension. On the other hand, he could not escape the fact that unless one believed that all communication was meaningless noise, every act of serious thinking and saying absolutely presupposes the possibility of truth. Even Nietzsche, the godless anti-metaphysician, comes to admit that he is "still too pious," that even he still worships at the altar where God's name is "truth":

But you will have gathered what I am driving at,
namely, that it is still a *metaphysical faith* upon
which our faith in science rests—that even we seekers after knowledge today, we godless anti-metaphysicians still take *our* fire, too, from the flame lit
by a faith that is thousands of years old, that
Christian faith, which was also the faith of Plato, that
God is the truth, that truth is divine.   [GS 344, 1887]

The Death of God

No aspect of Nietzsche's teaching is better known than
his announcement that "God is dead" ("The Death of
God"). The phrase actually conveys two Nietzschean convictions: first, that for reflective human beings the Judaeo-
Christian God is no longer credible; second, that the very
notion of a metaphysical world, a higher, more real world
from which this world derives, is equally fantastic.

Nietzsche called the death of God "the greatest
event in modern history" as well as the "cause of extreme
danger." We therefore misunderstand Nietzsche's attitude
unless we hear in these words—"the death of God"—
both Nietzsche's exultation and his horror. Exultation,
because Nietzsche, the prophet of new possibilities,
eagerly anticipates what humanity might become when it
"no longer flows out into a God."[1] The death of God is,
for him, the birth pang of a new humanity. But also horror, because this most sensitive religious thinker understands that since God has for so long been a constant in
the human soul, his demise marks a new and treacherous
phase of the human story, one that will witness nothing
less than "a transposition of valley and mountain such as
has never been dreamed of."[2] Only a vision that can

claim equally deep access to the human soul can fill the void left by God's departure. And that is a very tall order. That Nietzsche was far from sanguine about the terrible truth that God is dead is vividly conveyed in the words of the madman:

> [. . .] *We have killed him*—you and I. All of us are his murderers. But how have we done this? How were we able to drink up the sea? Who gave us the sponge to wipe away the entire horizon? What did we do when we unchained this earth from its sun? Whither is it moving now? Whither are we moving now? Away from all suns? Are we not plunging continually? [. . .] Are we not straying as through an infinite nothing? Do we not feel the breath of empty space? Has it not become colder? Is not night and more night coming on all the while? [. . .]

The Attack on Morality

All peoples everywhere have lived by codes of good and evil. Moralities—systems of evaluation—have been the great, invisible currents of history, propelling entire civilizations and reaching deeply into the psychic economy of individuals. Moral convictions exert an incomparable power over human affairs. Nietzsche's critique of morality, the subject of "The Immoralist", therefore lies at the very core of his radical revaluation of values.

Moralities generally derive their authority from the claim that they come not from man but from "above"—from God, the ancestors or the fabric of the universe. But if "God is dead," moralities can no longer make this claim. They are laid bare as human, all too human creations.

. . . Truly, men have given themselves all their good and evil. Truly, they did not take it, they did not find it, it did not descend to them as a voice from heaven.

Man first implanted values into things to maintain himself—he created the meaning of things, a human meaning! Therefore he calls himself: "Man", that is: the evaluator.3

We have divided Nietzsche's critique of morality into seven interrelated sections.

The Error of Free Will. Moral praise and moral condemnation presuppose that human beings are free to choose their courses of action. It is precisely this presupposition that Nietzsche rejects. For him, a human being is a piece of fate, not at all free as he or she supposes, but a reflex within a concatenation of physiological, psychological and socio-historical conditions. Praise and blame, reward and punishment, are actually meaningless. Human beings are no more accountable for their actions than water is for being wet. Human action is, in the last analysis, always and forever innocent. This insistence on the "innocence of becoming" is central to Nietzsche's own redemptive message: "[. . .] we deny accountability: only by doing *that* do we redeem the world."4

Morality as Anti-Nature. A philosophy based on the ineluctability of the will to power necessarily affirms the self-assertive quality of our life-instincts. Viewed from this angle, traditional morality, which often urges the blunting of self-assertion and a war against the passions, is actually an enemy of life. Therefore, though moralities have claimed to be the great engines of human *betterment*, they have actually, in Nietzsche's view, been the causes of humanity's decline and *décadence*. They have poisoned the actuality of human life with transcendental lies, made healthy instincts sick, and divided the self against itself.

The Absurdity of Altruism. Similarly, if life is the will to power, what is more unnatural, indeed more impossible, than selflessness? Nietzsche finds no evidence that there is any such thing as "unegoistic" action in nature. Self-interested action is the rule of life; only an animal bewildered by brainsick fantasies could miss this. "Not to seek one's own advantage" is pathetic advice given only by those who no longer know how to *find* their advantage.

The Folly of Pity. And again, if life is the will to power, what is more unnatural and inimical to life than pity for the weak and compassion for the unfortunate? Nietzsche suspects that pity, that great unquestioned virtue of so many moralities, is actually a vice. Pity drains energy, paralyses strength, multiplies misery.

Morality's Immoral Sources: Revenge and Ressentiment. Western morality is an outgrowth of diseased emotions. Its essential character was formed long ago, Nietzsche says, in a revolt of Jewish and Christian inferiors against their pagan superiors and has ever since been pervaded by feelings of resentment and revenge. "It's your fault that we are sick and you are healthy; it's your fault that we are plain and you are beautiful; it's your fault that we nibble at life while you feast! We will punish you!" The desire to blame and punish, to make others sick because one is sick oneself, sick *of* onself—this is the pathology of revenge that moral rhetoric conceals.

The Psychology of Guilt. The evolution from animal to man, and of civilization itself, required the persistent suppression of animal instincts and the invention of methods to keep that suppression in force. Chief among these inventions was psychic pain, the leaden discomfort of body and mind we call guilt. Priests of all stripes have been the great artists of guilt feelings, inventing elaborate fantasies about "God" and "sin" to justify and maintain the needed suppressions. But, says Nietzsche, "the bite of conscience, like the bite of a dog into a stone, is a stupidity."[5]

Herd Morality and the Lie of Equality. Because few things were as obvious to Nietzsche as the differences among human beings, the democratic premise—equal rights and equal duties for all—repulsed him. Equality is a lie concocted by inferior people who arrange themselves in herds to overpower those who are naturally superior to them. The morality of "equal rights" is herd morality, and because it opposes the cultivation of superior individuals, it leads to the corruption of the human species.

Against Christianity

"Christianity has been up till now mankind's greatest misfortune."[6] These words aptly convey the extremity of Nietzsche's attack on Christianity in which his opposition to western morality and theology comes, as it were, to a head. It is tempting to dismiss Nietzsche's anti-Christian polemic as deranged animosity, but this would be a mistake: "If I wage war on Christianity I have a right to do so, because I have never experienced anything disagreeable or frustrating from that direction—the most serious

Christians have always been well disposed towards me."7 Indeed we must remember that, for Nietzsche, life, and the intellectual life above all, is essentially agonistic. Nothing excellent is achieved without the effort inspired by conflict. The noble mind loves its enemies, not out of piety, but because the presence of enemies requires one to hone one's talents. For Nietzsche there was no greater enemy than Christianity and therefore, in this sense, no greater love. Nietzsche was not ungrateful: "But the struggle [. . .] against the Christian-ecclesiastical pressure of millennia [. . .] has created in Europe a magnificent tension of the spirit such as has never existed on earth before: with so tense a bow one can now shoot for the most distant targets. [. . .] we *good Europeans* and free, *very* free spirits—we have it still, the whole need of the spirit and the whole tension of its bow!"8

In *The Good News of Jesus*, Nietzsche explores the mind and heart of Jesus himself. There he finds the mystical awareness that "every kind of distancing relationship between God and man is abolished—precisely this is the *"glad tidings"*. Blessedness [. . .] is the *only* reality."9 In *Good News Gone Bad*, Nietzsche considers the ways in which early Christians, notably Paul, not fully free from old habits of thought and driven by all too human motives, distorted Jesus' message. In *Why Nietzsche Is Not A Christian*, an array of Christian ideas—God, sin, guilt, redemption, eternal life, grace —are subjected to a fierce psychological analysis.

The Free Spirit

What happens when one has cut oneself loose from all the moorings that Truth, God, and Morality have formerly provided? Indeed, what happens when, upon setting out

to sea, one finds that one has burned not only all bridges
but all the *land* as well, so that now there is nothing but
sea, sea, *sea*! Is this sea of freedom not terrifying in its
uncharted immensity? The two sections of "The Free
Spirit", The Open Sea and New Tasks, collect some of
the finest examples of Nietzsche's inspired rhetoric,
focussing on the fresh perspectives and daunting chal-
lenges that await philosophers and other free, *terribly*
free spirits as they gaze upon new and distant horizons.
"Now, little ship, take care!"[10]

Superman (The Higher Human Being)

"Nietzsche is not simply what we have thought— godless, an unbeliever, an immoralist—for these labels, while
correct, are inadequate because he is these things in such
an advanced form that, being mere negations, they cannot even hint at what is positive in his thought."
Nietzsche's philosophy "aims at nothing less than a spiritual renewal of the now global West."[11] "Higher
Humanity" takes us to the heart of Nietzsche's positive
vision, the figure of the Superman, clearly intended to fill
the void left by the death of God: "Once you said 'God'
[. . .]; but now I have taught you to say 'Superman'".[12]

The Superman (Section 1) is one: whose self-mastery yields an abundance of the power to create; who
exercises the master privilege of the free spirit—living
experimentally; who bids farewell to the reverences of
youth and who stands apart from the views and values
of the herd; who reverences enemies as allies;[13] who
knows how to forget and recuperate from the blows of
life; who shakes off with a single shrug the vermin that
eat deeply into others; whose overflowing plenitude and

gratitude cleanse both body and spirit of all guilt and all *ressentiment*; who perceives that "body" and "spirit" are two names for a single mystery; who calls humankind to return in love to its true home, the Earth; whose every muscle quivers with a proud consciousness of truly free will and a sovereign individuality[14] that "no longer flows out into a God";[15] who realizes that creative individuality is indeed the Earth's goal and humanity's hope; who, without metaphysical consolations, affirms life not only in its joy but in all its horror and who, thereby, conquers nihilism. Nietzsche exclaims: "this Antichrist and anti-nihilist; this victor over God and nothingness—*he must come one day.*"[16]

The Superman is shaped in the school of self-over-coming (Section 2) whose curriculum requires both courage and discipline, and above all, the ability to distinguish between an asceticism that denies life and one that stands in its service. The school of self-overcoming gives birth to the creative will (Section 3) and to a healthy, unrepentant selfishness (Section 4).

Joyful Wisdom

Nietzsche derides as "woeful wisdom" any view that rates life inferior to some supposed transcendental state. All such views—that is to say, almost all the great philosophies and religions of the human past—link life's meaning to fulfillment in an imaginary beyond. Nietzsche therefore finds implicit in such views a morbid No uttered against life as such. In response, he offers a redemptive Yes to life, a joyful wisdom. The six sections of "Joyful Wisdom" explore this affirmative mood.

Eternal Recurrence

Nietzsche defines the eternal recurrence (Section 1) as "the unconditional and endlessly repeated circular course of all things."[17] Having assumed that the past stretches backward to infinity, Nietzsche reasons that every possible configuration of the matter in the universe must have already occurred an infinite number of times. Everything that is happening now has happened before and will one day happen again in precisely the same way. The future has already been. All the greatness and triviality, all the joy and pain, all the delight and excruciating horror of all that has ever been will be again, forever, without alteration, without improvement, eternally without a meaning-giving End. If we asked some ghoul to give us a picture of the rankest absurdity, an image of the world as a deeply meaningless whole, he could hardly do better than to suggest the eternal recurrence. Yet Nietzsche calls it "the highest formula of affirmation that can possibly be attained."[18] He seems to offer it as a test of strength for would-be superpersons, a final exam in the school of self-overcoming. It is as if Nietzsche asks those who have cleansed theselves of all false consolations: "Can you now affirm the world in spite of its absurdity? Do you love your deepest joys enough to want them for an eternity? And if so, do you understand that you must also embrace all the horrors with which they are eternally bound up? So can you, for the sake of your eternity-thirsting joys utter an eternal Yes to the world and thereby give your *own* meaning to a process that is devoid of one?[19]

Redemption (Section 2) resides in this sacred Yes and in *amor fati* (love of fate), a Nietzschean formula that is synonymous with affirmation of the recurrence. To love fate is to bless everything that is as it is. It is a recognition that one is but an aspect of an immeasureably complex whole that cannot be otherwise. This insight restores innocence to all becoming. Thus does it redeem the world. The primary symbol of Nietzsche's redemptive-affirmative vision is the god Dionysus (Section 3). The Dionysian spirit lives in the full-blooded embrace of life in all its darkness and light, terror and joy.

Nietzsche's joyful wisdom also reclaims the body as a spiritual ally (Section 4) and teaches that the Earth is our true, because our only, spiritual home (Section 5). Finally, joyful wisdom defeats the nausea of despair. In the images of Nietzsche's arresting parable, it is as if one awoke to find a snake bitten deep into one's throat. Who has the courage to bite off its venomous head and spit it away to arise transformed? Radiant? *Laughing*?

---

[1] GS 285.

[2] EH *Why I Am A Destiny* 1.

[3] Z I *Of the Thousand and One Goals*.

[4] T *Four Great Errors* 8.

[5] WS 38.

[6] A 51.

[7] EH *Why I Am So Wise* 7.

[8] BGE Preface.

[9] A 33.

[10] GS 124.

[11] Lampert, *Nietzsche and Modern Times*, New Haven and London, Yale University Press, 1993, 328, 330, 280.

[12] Z II *On the Blissful Islands*.

[13] GM 1.10.

[14] GM 2.2.

[15] GS 285.

[16] GM 2.24.

[17] EH *The Birth of Tragedy* 3.

[18] EH *Thus Spake Zarathustra* 1.

[19] The ethical imperative (say "yes"!) lodged within the doctrine of the eternal recurrence presupposes the very freedom of choice that the recurrence itself denies. This is only the beginning of the logical morass into which the doctrine leads. Nietzsche's hope for the future and his calls for the evolution of the Superman are rendered absurd by it. Not all scholars agree, however, that the recurrence means "repetition of the same." H. Tomlinson's introduction to G. Deleuze's highly regarded *Nietzsche and Philosophy*, N.Y., Columbia University Press, 1983, calls this interpretation "childish". But it is difficult to see why, since Nietzsche's own formulations seem to say exactly that.

PART TWO
Selections from
Nietzsche's Writings

Preface:
Nietzsche's
Request To
His Readers

1

It is not for nothing that one has been a philologist, perhaps one is a philologist still, that is to say, a teacher of
slow reading [. . .] Nowadays it is not only my habit, it is
also to my taste [. . .] no longer to write anything which
does not reduce to despair every sort of man who is 'in a
hurry'. For philology is that venerable art which demands
of its votaries one thing above all: to go aside, to take
time, to become still, to become slow—it is a goldsmith's
art and connoisseurship of the *word* which has nothing
but delicate, cautious work to do and achieves nothing if
it does not achieve it *lento*. But for precisely this reason it
is more necessary than ever today, by precisely this
means does it entice and enchant us the most, in the
midst of an age of "work", that is to say, of hurry, of
indecent and perspiring haste, which wants to "get everything done" at once, including every old or new
book:—this art does not so easily get anything done, it

teaches to read *well*, that is to say, to read slowly, deeply, looking cautiously before and aft, with reservations, with doors left open, with delicate eyes and fingers . . . My patient friends, this book desires for itself only perfect readers and philologists: *learn* to read me well!

[D *Preface* (1886)]

The Fulcrum

[. . .] where life is, there is also will: not will to life, but—so I teach you—will to power!

1 Z II *Of Self-Overcoming*

Will to Power

2

What we are most subtle in.—Because for many thousands of years one thought that *things* (nature, tools, property of all kinds) were also alive and animate, with the power to cause harm and to evade human purposes, the feeling of impotence has been much greater and much more common among men than it would otherwise have been: for one needed to secure oneself against things, just as against men and animals, by force, constraint, flattering, treaties, sacrifices—and here is the origin of most superstitious practices, that is to say, of a considerable, *perhaps preponderant* and yet wasted and useless constituent of all the activity hitherto pursued by man!—But because the feeling of impotence and fear was in a state of almost continuous stimulation so strongly and for so long, the *feeling of power* has evolved to such a degree of *subtlety* that in this respect man is now a match for the most delicate goldbalance. It has become his strongest propensity; the means discovered for creating this feeling almost constitute the history of culture.

[D 23]

3

The striving for distinction.—The striving for distinction keeps a constant eye on the next man and wants to know what his feelings are: but the empathy which this drive requires for its gratification is far from being harmless or sympathetic or kind. We want, rather, to perceive or divine how the next man outwardly or inwardly *suffers* from us, how he loses control over himself and surrenders to the impressions our hand or even merely the sight of us makes upon him; and even when he who strives after distinction makes and wants to make a joyful, elevating or cheering impression, he nonetheless enjoys this success not inasmuch as he has given joy to the next man or elevated or cheered him, but inasmuch as he has *impressed* himself on the soul of the other, changed its shape and ruled over it at his own sweet will. The striving for distinction is the striving for domination over the next man, though it be a very indirect domination and only felt or even dreamed. There is a long scale of degrees of this secretly desired domination, and a complete catalogue of them would be almost the same thing as a history of culture [. . .]

[D 113]

4

Danae and God in gold.—Whence comes this immoderate impatience which nowadays turns a man into a criminal under circumstances which would be more compatible with an opposite tendency? For if one man employ false weights, another burns his house down after he has insured it for a large sum, a third counterfeits false coins, if three-quarters of the upper classes indulge in permitted fraud and have the stock exchange and speculations on their conscience: what drives them? Not actual need, for they are not so badly off, perhaps they even eat and drink without a care—but they are afflicted day and night by a fearful impatience at the slow way with which their money is accumulating and by an equally fearful pleasure in and love of accumulated money. In this impatience and this love, however, there turns up again that fanaticism of the *lust for power* which was in former times inflamed by the belief one was in possession of the truth and which bore such beautiful names that one could thenceforward venture to be inhuman *with a good conscience* (to burn Jews, heretics and good books and exterminate entire higher cultures such as those of Peru and Mexico). The means employed by the lust for power have changed, but the same volcano continues to glow, the impatience and the immoderate love demand their sacrifice: and what one formerly did 'for the sake of God' one now does for the sake of money, that is to say, for the sake of that which *now* gives the highest feeling of power and good conscience.

[D 204]

5

Effect of happiness.—The first effect of happiness is the *feeling of power*: this wants to *express itself*, either to us ourselves, or to other men, or to ideas or imaginary beings. The most common modes of expression are: to bestow, to mock, to destroy—all three out of a common basic drive.

[D 356]

6

On the theory of the feeling of power.—By doing good
and doing ill one exercises one's power upon
others—more one does not want! By *doing ill* upon
those to whom we first have to make our power palpable [. . .] By *doing good* and well-wishing upon those
who are in some way already dependent upon us [. . .]
Whether we make a sacrifice in doing good or ill does
not alter the ultimate value of our actions; even if we
stake our life, as the martyr does for the sake of his
Church—it is a sacrifice to *our* desire for power or for
the purpose of preserving our feeling of power. He who
feels 'I am in possession of the truth', how many posses-
sions does he not let go in order to rescue this sensation!
What does he not throw overboard in order to remain
'aloft'—that is to say, *above* others who lack the 'truth'!
Certainly, the condition in which we do ill is seldom as
pleasant, as unmixedly pleasant, as that in which we do
good—it is a sign that we still lack power [. . .]

[GS 13]

7

What urges you on and arouses your ardour, you wisest
of men, do you call it 'will to truth'?

[. . .] it is a will to power; and that is so even when
you talk of good and evil and of the assessment of
values.

You want to create the world before which you can
kneel: this is your ultimate hope and intoxication. [. . .]

Where I found a living creature, there I found will to
power; and even in the will of the servant I found the
will to be master.

The will of the weaker persuades it to serve the stronger; its will wants to be master over those weaker still: this delight alone it is unwilling to forgo. [. . .]

And life itself told me this secret: 'Behold,' it said, 'I am that *which must overcome itself again and again*.

'To be sure, you call it will to procreate or impulse towards a goal, towards the higher, more distant, more manifold: but all this is one and one secret.

'I would rather perish than renounce this one thing; and truly, where there is perishing and the falling of leaves, behold, there life sacrifices itself—for the sake of power! [. . .]

'And you too, enlightened man, are only a path and footstep of my will: truly, my will to power walks with the feet of your will to truth!

'He who shot the doctrine of "will to existence" at truth certainly did not hit the truth: this will—does not exist!

'For what does not exist cannot will; but that which is in existence, how could it still want to come into existence?

'Only where life is, there is also will: not will to life, but—so I teach you—will to power!

'The living creature values many things higher than life itself; yet out of this evaluation itself speaks—the will to power!' [. . .]

[Z II *Of Self-Overcoming*]

8

[. . .] [W]hat formerly happened with the Stoics still happens today as soon as a philosophy begins to believe in itself. It always creates the world in its own image, it

cannot do otherwise; philosophy is this tyrannical drive
itself, the most ·spiritual will to power, to 'creation of the
world', to *causa prima*.

[BGE 9]

9

Physiologists should think again before postulating the
drive to self-preservation as the cardinal drive in an
organic being. A living thing desires above all to *vent* its
strength—life as such is will to power—: self-preservation is only one of the indirect and most frequent *consequences* of it. [. . .]

[BGE 13]

10

All psychology has hitherto remained anchored to moral
prejudices and timidities: it has not ventured into the
depths. To conceive it as morphology and the *develop-
ment-theory of the will to power*, as I conceive it—has
never yet so much as entered the mind of anyone else
[. . .]

[BGE 23]

11

Granted that nothing is 'given' as real except our world of
desires and passions, that we can rise or sink to no other
'reality' than the reality of our drives—for thinking is only
the relationship of these drives to one another: is it not
permitted to make the experiment and ask the question
whether this which is given does not *suffice* for an understanding even of the so-called mechanical (or 'material')
world? I do not mean as a deception, an 'appearance', an
'idea' (in the Berkeleyan and Schopenhauerin sense),

but as possessing the same degree of reality as our emotions themselves—as a more primitive form of the world of emotions in which everything still lies locked in mighty unity and then branches out and develops in the organic process [. . .] as a kind of instinctual life in which all organic functions, together with self-regulation, assimilation, nourishment, excretion, metabolism, are still synthetically bound together—as an *antecedent form* of life? [. . .] In the end, the question is whether we really recognize will as *efficient*, whether we believe in the causality of will: if we do—and fundamentally belief in *this* is precisely our belief in causality itself—then we *have* to make the experiment of positing causality of will hypothetically as the only one. 'Will' can of course operate only on 'will'—and not on 'matter' (not on 'nerves', for example—): enough, one must venture the hypothesis that wherever 'effects' are recognized, will is operating upon will—Granted finally that one succeeded in explaining our entire instinctual life as the development and ramification of *one* basic form of will—as will to power, as is *my* theory—; granted that one could trace all organic functions back to this will to power and could also find in it the solution to the problem of procreation and nourishment—they are *one* problem—one would have acquired the right to define *all* efficient force unequivocally as: *will to power*. The world seen from within, the world described and defined according to its 'intelligible character'—it would be 'will to power' and nothing else.

[BGE 36]

12

To refrain from mutual injury, mutual violence, mutual exploitation, to equate one's own will with that of another: this may in a certain rough sense become good manners between individuals if the conditions for it are present (namely if their strength and value standards are in fact similar and they both belong to *one* body). As soon as there is a desire to take this principle further, however, and if possible even as the *fundamental principle of society*, it at once reveals itself for what it is: as the will to the *denial* of life, as the principle of dissolution and decay. One has to think this matter thoroughly through to the bottom and resist all sentimental weakness: life itself is *essentially* appropriation, injury, overpowering of the strange and weaker, suppression, severity, imposition of one's own forms, incorporation and, at the least and mildest, exploitation—but why should one always have to employ precisely those words which have from of old been stamped with a slanderous intention? Even that body within which [. . .] individuals treat one another as equals [. . .] must, if it is a living and not a decaying body, [. . .] want to grow, expand, draw to itself, gain ascendancy—not out of any morality or immorality, but because it *lives*, and because life *is* will to power. On no point, however, is the common European consciousness more reluctant to learn than it is here; everywhere one enthuses, even under scientific disguises, about coming states of society in which there will be 'no more exploitation'—that sounds to my ears like promising a life in which there will be no organic functions. 'Exploitation' does not pertain to a corrupt or imperfect or primitive society: it pertains to the *essence* of the living thing as a fundamental organic function, it is a

consequence of the intrinsic will to power which is precisely the will of life.—Granted this is a novelty as a theory—as a reality it is the *primordial fact* of all history: let
us be at least that honest with ourselves!

[BGE 259]

13

[. . .] To want to preserve oneself is the expression of a
state of distress, a limitation of the actual basic drive of
life, which aims at *extension of power* and in obedience
to this will often enough calls self-preservation into question and sacrifices it. [. . .] in nature the *rule* is not the
state of distress, it is superfluity, prodigality, even to the
point of absurdity. The struggle for existence is only an
exception, a temporary restriction of the will of life; the
struggle, great and small, everywhere turns on ascendancy, on growth and extension, in accordance will the will
to power, which is precisely the will of life.

[GS 349 (1887)]

14

[. . .] No matter how well one may have understood the
utility of some physiological organ (or of a legal institu-
tion, a social custom, a political usage, a form in the arts
or in the religious cult) one has not therewith understood
anything in regard to its origin [. . .] all objectives, all util-
ities are only *signs* that a will to power has become master of something less powerful and has imprinted upon it
the sense of a function; and the entire history of a 'thing',
an organ, a usage can in this way be a continuing chain
of signs of ever new interpretations and arrangements
whose causes themselves do not have to be connected
with one another but rather in some cases merely follow

and replace one another by chance. [. . .] Things are no different even within an individual organism: with every essential growth of the whole the 'meaning' of the individual organs is shifted—in some cases their partial destruction or a reduction in their numbers [. . .] can be a sign of increasing strength and perfection. I mean to say: even a partial *becoming useless*, an atrophying and degeneration, a loss of meaning and purposiveness, in short death, is among the conditions of actual *progressus*; and this always appears in the form of a will and way to *greater power*, and is always carried through at the expense of numerous smaller powers. [. . .]

[GM 2.12]

15

What is good?—All that heightens the feeling of power, the will to power, power itself in man.

What is bad?—All that proceeds from weakness.

What is happiness?—The feeling that power *increases*—that a resistance is overcome. [. . .]

[A 2]

The Destroyer

He who has to be a creator always has to destroy.
[Z I *Of a Thousand and One Goals*]

And let everything that can break upon our truths—break! There is many a house still to build!
[Z II *Of Self-Overcoming*]

"What are you really doing, erecting an ideal or knocking one down?" I may perhaps be asked. [. . .] If a temple is to be erected *a temple must be destroyed:* that is the law [. . .] !
[GM 2:24]

I am not a man, I am dynamite.
[EH *Why I Am A Destiny* 1]

The Labyrinth
of Truth

16

In some remote corner of the universe, poured out and glittering in innumerable solar systems, there once was a star on which clever animals invented knowledge. That was the haughtiest and most mendacious minute of "world history"—yet only a minute. After nature had drawn a few breaths the star grew cold, and the clever animals had to die.

One might invent such a fable and still not have illustrated sufficiently how wretched, how shadowy and flighty, how aimless and arbitrary, the human intellect appears in nature. There have been eternities when it did not exist; and when it is done for again, nothing will have happened. For this intellect has no further mission that would lead beyond human life. It is human, rather, and only its owner and producer gives it such importance, as if the world pivoted around it. But if we could communicate with the mosquito, then we would learn that it floats through the air with the same self-importance, feeling within itself the flying center of the world. [. . .]

The intellect, as a means for the preservation of the
individual, unfolds its chief powers in simulation; for this
is the means by which the weaker, less robust individuals
preserve themselves [. . .]: here deception, flattery, lying
and cheating, talking behind the back, [. . .] acting a role
before others and before oneself [. . .] is so much the rule
[. . .] that almost nothing is more incomprehensible than
how an honest and pure urge for truth could make its
appearance among men. [. . .]

What, indeed, does man know of himself! [. . .] Does
not nature keep much the most from him, even about his
body, to spellbind and confine him in a proud, deceptive
consciousness, far from the coils of the intestines, the
quick current of the blood stream, and the involved
tremors of the fibers? She threw away the key; and woe
to the calamitous curiosity which might peer just once
through a crack in the chamber of consciousness and
look down, and sense that man rests upon the merciless,
the greedy, the insatiable, the murderous, in the difference of his ignorance—hanging in dreams, as it were,
upon the back of a tiger. In view of this, whence in all
the world comes the urge for truth? [. . .]

What, then, is truth? A mobile army of metaphors,
metonyms, and anthropomorphisms—in short, a sum of
human relations, which have been enhanced, trans-
posed, and embellished poetically and rhetorically, and
which after long use seem firm, canonical, and obligatory
to a people: truths are illusions about which one has for-
gotten that this is what they are; metaphors which are
worn out and without sensuous power; coins which have
lost their pictures and now matter only as metal, no
longer as coins.

We still do not know where the urge for truth comes
from; for as yet we have heard only of the obligation

imposed by society that it should exist: to be truthful means using the customary metaphors—in moral terms: the obligation to lie according to a fixed convention, to lie herd-like in a style obligatory for all [. . .]

[from *On Truth and Lie In an Extra Moral Sense*]¹

17

Family failing of philosophers.—All philosophers have the common failing of starting out from man as he is now and thinking they can reach their goal through an analysis of him. They involuntarily think of 'man' as an *aeterna veritas*, as something that remains constant in the midst of all flux, as a sure measure of things. Everything the philosopher has declared about man is, however, at bottom no more than a testimony as to the man of a *very limited* period of time. Lack of historical sense is the family failing of all philosophers; many, without being aware of it, even take the most recent manifestation of man, such as has arisen under the impress of certain religions, even certain political events, as the fixed form from which one has to start out. They will not learn that man has become, that the faculty of cognition has become; while some of them would have it that the whole world is spun out of this faculty of cognition. Now, everything *essential* in the development of mankind took place in primeval times, long before the 4,000 years we more or less know about; during these years mankind may well not have altered very much. But the philosopher here sees 'instincts' in man as he now is and assumes that these belong to the unalterable facts of mankind, and to that extent could provide a key to the understanding of the world in general: the whole of teleology is constructed by speaking of the man of the last four millennia as of an *eternal* man towards whom all the things in the world have had a natural relationship from the time he began. But everything has become: there are *no eternal facts*, just as there are no absolute truths. Consequently what is needed from now on is *historical philosophizing*, and with it the virtue of modesty.

[HA 2]

18

Language as putative science. [. . .] To the extent that man has for long ages believed in the concepts and names of things as in *aeternae veritates* he has appropriated to himself that pride by which he raised himself above the animal: he really thought that in language he possessed knowledge of the world. The sculptor of language was not so modest as to believe that he was only giving things designations, he conceived rather that with words he was expressing supreme knowledge of things; [. . .] Here, too, it is the *belief that the truth has been found* out of which the mightiest sources of energy have flowed. Very much subsequently—only now—it dawns on men that in their belief in language they have propagated a tremendous error. Happily, it is too late for the evolution of reason, which depends on this belief, to be again put back. [. . .]

[HA 11]

19

Fundamental insight.—There is no pre-established harmony between the furtherance of truth and the well-being of mankind.

[HA 517]

20

Ultimate scepticism.—What then in the last resort are the truths of mankind?—They are the *irrefutable* errors of mankind.

[GS 265]

21

[. . .] most of a philosopher's conscious thinking is secretly directed and compelled into definite channels by his instincts. Behind all logic too and its apparent autonomy there stand evaluations, in plainer terms physiological demands for the preservation of a certain species of life.

[BGE 3]

22

The falseness of a judgement is to us not necessarily an objection to a judgement: it is here that our new language perhaps sounds strangest. The question is to what extent it is life-advancing, life-preserving, [. . .] and our fundamental tendency is to assert that the falsest judgements [. . .] are the most indispensable to us, that without granting as true the fictions of logic, without measuring reality against the purely invented world of the unconditional and self-identical, without a continual falsification of the world by means of numbers, mankind could not live—that to renounce false judgements would be to renounce life, would be to deny life. To recognize truth as a condition of life: that, to be sure, means to resist customary value-sentiments in a dangerous fashion; and a philosophy which ventures to do so places itself, by that act alone, beyond good and evil.

[BGE 4]

23

It has gradually become clear to me what every great
philosophy has hitherto been: a confession on the part of
its author and a kind of involuntary and unconscious
memoir; moreover, that the moral (or immoral) intentions
in every philosophy have every time constituted the real
germ of life out of which the entire plant has grown. To
explain how a philosopher's most remote metaphysical
assertions have actually been arrived at, it is always well
(and wise) to ask oneself first: what morality does this
(does *he*—) aim at?

[BGE 6]

24

[. . .] the philosopher, as the creature which has hitherto
always been most fooled on earth, has by now a *right* to
'bad character'—he has today the *duty* to be distrustful,
to squint wickedly up out of every abyss of suspicion.
[. . .] Why *not*? It is no more than a moral prejudice that
truth is worth more than appearance; it is even the worst-
proved assumption that exists. [. . .] Indeed, what compels us to assume there exists any essential antithesis
between 'true' and 'false'? Is it not enough to suppose
grades of apparentness and as it were lighter and darker
shades and tones of appearance—different *valeurs*, to
speak in the language of painters? [. . .]

[BGE 34]

25

[. . .] we are from the very heart and from the very first—
accustomed to lying. Or, to express it more virtuously
and hypocritically, in short more pleasantly: one is much
more of an artist than one realizes. [. . .]

[BGE 192]

26

[. . .] does one not write books precisely to conceal what lies within us?—indeed, [one] will doubt whether a philosopher *could* have 'final and real' opinions at all, whether behind each of his caves there does not and must not lie another, deeper cave—a stranger, more comprehensive world beyond the surface, an abyss behind every ground, beneath every 'foundation'. Every philosophy is a foreground philosophy [. . .] Every philosophy also *conceals* a philosophy; every opinion is also a hiding-place, every word also a mask.

[BGE 289]

27

How we, too, are still pious.—In science convictions have no rights of citizenship [. . .]. Only when they descend to the modesty of hypotheses [. . .] they may be granted admission and even a certain value in the realm of knowledge [. . .].—But does this not mean [. . .] that a conviction may obtain admission to science only when it *ceases* to be a conviction? Would it not be the first step in the discipline of the scientific spirit that one would not permit oneself any more convictions?

Probably this is so; only we still have to ask: *To make it possible for this discipline to begin*, must there not be some prior conviction—even one that is so commanding and unconditional that it sacrifices all other convictions to itself? We see that science also rests on a faith; there simply is no science "without presuppositions." The question whether *truth* is needed must not only have been affirmed in advance, but affirmed to such a degree that the principle, the faith, the conviction finds expression: '*Nothing* is needed *more* than truth, and in relation to it everything else has only second-rate value.'

This unconditional will to truth—what is it? [. . .]
What do you know in advance of the character of existence, to be able to decide whether the greater advantage is on the side of the unconditionally mistrustful or of
the unconditionally trusting? But if both should be
required, much trust *as well as* much mistrust, from
where would science then be permitted to take its
unconditional faith or conviction on which it rests, that
truth is more important than any other thing, including
every other conviction? Precisely this conviction could
never have come into being if both truth and untruth
constantly proved to be useful, which is the case.
Thus—the faith in science, which after all exists undeni-
ably, cannot owe its origin to such a calculus of utility; it
must have originated *in spite of* the fact that the disutility
and dangerousness of "the will to truth," of "truth at any
price," is proved to it constantly. "At any price": how well
we understand these words once we have offered and
slaughtered one faith after another on this altar!

Consequently, "will to truth" does *not* mean "I will
not allow myself to be deceived" but—there is no alternative—"I will not deceive, not even myself"; *and with
that we stand on moral ground.* For you only have to ask
yourself carefully, "Why do you not want to deceive?"
especially if it should seem—and it does seem!—as if life
aimed at semblance, meaning error, deception, simulation, delusion, self-delusion, [. . .]

Thus the question "Why science?" leads back to the
moral problem, *Why have morality at all* when life,
nature, and history are "not moral"? No doubt, those who
are truthful in that audacious and ultimate sense that is
presupposed by the faith in science *thus affirm another
world* than the world of life, nature, and history; and
insofar as they affirm this "other world"—look, must they

not by the same token negate its counterpart, this world, *our* world?—But you will have gathered what I am driving at, namely, that it is still a *metaphysical faith* upon which our faith in science rests—that even we seekers after knowledge today, we godless anti-metaphysicians still take our fire, too, from the flame lit by a faith that is thousands of years old, that Christian faith which was also the faith of Plato, that God is the truth, that truth is divine. [. . .]

[GS 344 (1887)]

28

[. . .] There is *only* a perspective seeing, *only* a perspective "knowing" [. . .]

[GM 3.12]

29

[. . .] These Nay-sayers and outsiders of today who are unconditional on one point—their insistence on intellectual cleanliness; [. . .] all these pale atheists, anti-Christians, immoralists, nihilists; these skeptics [. . .]; they certainly believe they are as completely liberated from the ascetic ideal as possible, these "free, *very* free spirits"; and yet, to disclose to them what they themselves cannot see [. . .]: this ideal is precisely *their* ideal, too; they themselves embody it today and perhaps they alone; they themselves are its most spiritualized product, its most advanced front-line troops and scouts, its most captious, tender, intangible form of seduction—if I have guessed any riddles, I wish that *this* proposition might show it!—They are far from being *free* spirits: *for they still have faith in truth.*

[. . .] it is precisely in their faith in truth that they are more rigid and unconditional than anyone. I know all this from too close up perhaps: that venerable philosopher's abstinence to which such a faith commits one; that intellectual stoicism which ultimately refuses not only to affirm but also to deny; that *desire* to halt before the factual [. . .]—all this expresses, broadly speaking, as much ascetic virtue as any denial of sensuality (it is at bottom only a particular mode of this denial). That which *constrains* these men, however, this unconditional will to truth, is *faith in the ascetic ideal itself*, even if as an unconscious imperative—don't be deceived about that—it is the faith in a *metaphysical* value, the absolute value of *truth*, sanctioned and guaranteed by this ideal alone (it stands or falls with this ideal).

[. . .] The will to truth requires a critique—let us thus define our own task—the value of truth must for once be experimentally *called into question*.

[GM 3.24]

30

[. . .] Everywhere else that the spirit is strong, mighty, and at work without counterfeit today, it does without ideals of any kind—the popular expression for this abstinence is "atheism"—*except for its will to truth*. But this will, this *remnant* of an ideal, is, if you will believe me, this ideal itself in its strictest, most spiritual formulation, esoteric through and through, with all external additions abolished, and thus not so much its remnant as its *kernel*. Unconditional honest atheism (and *its* is the only air we breathe, we more spiritual men of this age!) is therefore *not* the antithesis of that ideal, as it appears to be; it is rather only one of the latest phases of its evolution, one of its terminal forms and inner consequences—it is the awe-inspiring *catastrophe* of two-thousand years of training in truthfulness that finally forbids itself the *lie involved in belief in God*. [. . .]

What, in all strictness, has really *conquered* the Christian God? The answer may be found in my *Gay Science* (section 357): "Christian morality itself, the concept of truthfulness taken more and more strictly [. . .]. To view nature as if it were a proof of the goodness and providence of a God; to interpret history to the glory of a divine reason, as the perpetual witness to a moral world order and moral intentions; to interpret one's own experiences, as pious men long interpreted them, as if everything were preordained, everything a sign, everything sent for the salvation of the soul—that now belong to the *past*, that has the conscience *against* it, that seems to every more sensitive conscience indecent, dishonest, mendacious [. . .]: it is this rigor if anything that makes us *good Europeans* and the heirs of Europe's longest and bravest self-overcoming."

All great things bring about their own destruction through an act of self-overcoming: thus the law of life will have it [. . .] In this way Christianity *as a dogma* was destroyed by its own morality; in the same way Christianity *as morality* must now perish, too: we stand on the threshold of *this* event. After Christian truthfulness has drawn one inference after another, it must end by drawing its *most striking inference*, its inference *against* itself; this will happen, however, when it poses the question *"what is the meaning of all will to truth?"*

And here I again touch on my problem, on our problem, my *unknown* friends (for as yet I *know* of no friend): what meaning would our whole being possess if it were not this, that in us the will to truth becomes conscious of itself as a *problem*?

As the will to truth thus gains self-consciousness—there can be no doubt of that—morality will gradually *perish* now: this is the great spectacle in a hundred acts reserved for the next two centuries in Europe—the most terrible, most questionable, and perhaps also the most hopeful of all spectacles.—

[GM 3.27]

31

One should not let oneself be misled: great intellects are sceptics. [. . .] The vigour of a mind, its *freedom* through strength and superior strength, is *proved* by scepticism. [. . .] Convictions are prisons. [. . .]

[A 54]

32

[. . .] I call a lie: wanting *not* to see something one does see, wanting not to see something *as* one sees it: whether the lie takes place before witnesses or without witnesses is of no consequence. The most common lie is the lie one tells to oneself; lying to others is relatively the exception.—Now this desiring *not* to see what one sees, this desiring not to see as one sees, is virtually the primary condition for all who are in any sense *party* : the party man necessarily becomes a liar. [. . .]

The 'Law', the 'will of God', the 'sacred book', 'inspiration'—all merely words for the conditions *under* which the priest comes to power, *by* which he maintains his power—these concepts are to be found at the basis of all priestly organizations, all priestly or priestly-philosophical power-structures. The 'holy lie'—common to Confucius, the Law-Book of Manu, Mohammed, the Christian Church—: it is not lacking in Plato. 'The truth exists': this means, wherever it is heard, *the priest is lying* . . .

[A 55]

33

He who knows how to breathe the air of my writings knows that it is an air of the heights, a *robust* air. One has to be made for it, otherwise there is no small danger one will catch cold. The ice is near, the solitude is terrible—but how peacefully all things lie in the light! how freely one breathes! how much one feels *beneath* one!—Philosophy, as I have hitherto understood and lived it, is a voluntary living in ice and high mountains—a seeking after everything strange and questionable in existence, all that has hitherto been excommunicated by morality. From the lengthy experience afforded by such a wandering in the *forbidden* I learned to view the origin of moralizing and idealizing very differently from what might be desirable: the *hidden* history of the philosophers, the psychology of their great names came to light for me.—How much truth can a spirit *bear*, how much truth can a spirit *dare*? that became for me more and more the real measure of value. [. . .]

[EH *Foreword* 3]

---

¹ In Walter Kaufmann, *The Portable Nietzsche*, New York Viking Press, 1954, 1968, 42–7.

The Death
of God

34

Misunderstanding of the dream.—The man of the ages of
barbarous primordial culture believed that in the dream
he was getting to know a *second real world*: here is the
origin of all metaphysics. Without the dream, one would
have had no occasion to divide the world into two. The
dissection into soul and body is also connected with the
oldest idea of the dream, likewise the postulation of a life
of the soul, thus the origin of all belief in spirits and
probably also of the belief in gods. 'The dead live on, *for*
they appear to the living in dreams': that was the conclusion one formerly drew, throughout many millennia.

[HA 5]

35

Metaphysical world.—It is true, there could be a metaphysical world; the absolute possibility of it is hardly to
be disputed. [. . .] [B]ut one can do absolutely nothing
with it, not to speak of letting happiness, salvation and
life depend on the gossamer of such a possibility.—For
one could assert nothing at all of the metaphysical world

except that it was a being-other, an inaccessible, incomprehensible being-other; it would be a thing with negative qualities.—Even if the existence of such a world were never so well demonstrated, it is certain that knowledge of it would be the most useless of all knowledge: more useless even than knowledge of the chemical composition of water must be to the sailor in danger of shipwreck.

[HA 9]

36

Appearance and thing-in-itself.—Philosophers are accustomed to place themselves before life and experience [. . .] as if before a painting that has been unrolled once and for all and unchangingly displays almost the same event: this event, they think, must be interpreted correctly in order to draw a conclusion as to the being which produced the painting: that is to say, as to the thing-in-itself, which is seen as the sufficient reason for the world of appearance. More rigorous logicians, on the other hand, after they had strictly established the concept of the metaphysical as that of the unconditioned, consequently also the unconditioning, denied any connection between the unconditioned (the metaphysical world) and the world known to us: so that what appears in appearance is precisely not the thing-in-itself, and any conclusion from the former to the latter is to be rejected. Both parties, however, overlook the possibility that this painting—that which we men call life and experience—has gradually *become*, is indeed still fully in process of *becoming*, and should thus not be regarded as a fixed magnitude from which one might draw a conclusion as to the originator (the sufficient reason) or even reject such a conclusion. [. . .] That which we now call the world is the result of a host of errors and fantasies which have gradually arisen in the course of the total evolution of organic nature, have become entwined with one another and are now inherited by us as the accumulated treasure of the entire past—as a treasure: for the value of our humanity depends on it. Rigorous science is in fact able to detach us from this ideational world only to a slight extent [. . .] but it can gradually and step by step illuminate the history of how this world as idea arose—and raise us above the whole thing at least for moments at a time. Perhaps we then recognize that the thing-in-itself is worthy of Homeric laughter: it *appeared* to be so much, indeed everything, and is actually empty, that is to say empty of meaning.

[HA 16]

37

Art makes the thinker's heart heavy.—How strong the metaphysical need is, and how hard nature makes it to bid it a final farewell, can be seen from the fact that even when the free spirit has divested himself of everything metaphysical the highest effects of art can easily set the metaphysical strings, which have long been silent or indeed snapped apart, vibrating in sympathy. [. . .] If he becomes aware of being in this condition he feels a profound stab in the heart and sighs for the man who will lead him back to his lost love, whether she be called religion or metaphysics. It is in such moments that his intellectual probity is put to the test.

[HA 153]

38

The Beyond in art.—It is not without profound sorrow that one admits to oneself that in their highest flights the

artists of all ages have raised to heavenly transfiguration
precisely those conceptions which we now recognize as
false: they are the glorifiers of the religious and philosophical errors of mankind, and they could not have
been so without believing in the absolute truth of these
errors. If belief in such truth declines in general [. . .] that
species of art can never flourish again which, like the
Divina Commedia, the pictures of Raphael, the frescoes
of Michelangelo, the Gothic cathedrals, presupposes not
only a cosmic but also a metaphysical significance in the
objects of art. A moving tale will one day be told how
there once existed such an art, such an artist's faith.

[HA 220]

39

New struggles.—After Buddha was dead, his shadow was
still shown for centuries in a cave—a tremendous, grue-
some shadow. God is dead; but given the way of men,
there may still be caves for thousands of years in which
his shadow will be shown.—And we—we still have to
vanquish his shadow, too.

[GS 108]

40

The madman.—Have you not heard of that madman
who lit a lantern in the bright morning hours, ran to the
market-place and cried incessantly: 'I am looking for
God! I am looking for God!'—As many of those who did
not believe in God were standing together there he excited considerable laughter. Have you lost him then? said
one. Did he lose his way like a child? said another. Or is
he hiding? Is he afraid of us? Has he gone on a voyage?
Or emigrated?—thus they shouted and laughed. The
madman sprang into their midst and pierced them with

his glances. 'Where has God gone?' he cried. 'I shall tell you. *We have killed him*—you and I. We are all his murderers. But how have we done this? How were we able to drink up the sea? Who gave us the sponge to wipe away the entire horizon? What did we do when we unchained this earth from its sun? Whither is it moving now? Whither are we moving now? Away from all suns? Are we not perpetually falling? Backward, sideward, forward, in all directions? Is there any up or down left? Are we not straying as through an infinite nothing? Do we not feel the breath of empty space? Has it not become colder? Is more and more night not coming on all the time? Must not lanterns be lit in the morning? Do we not hear anything yet of the noise of the gravediggers who are burying God? Do we not smell anything yet of God's decomposition?—gods, too, decompose. God is dead. God remains dead. And we have killed him. How shall we, the murderers of all murderers, console ourselves? That which was holiest and mightiest of all that the world has yet possessed has bled to death under our knives—who will wipe this blood off us? With what water could we purify ourselves? What festivals of atonement, what sacred games shall we need to invent? Is not the greatness of this deed too great for us? Must we not ourselves become gods simply to seem worthy of it? There has never been a greater deed—and whoever shall be born after us, for the sake of this deed he shall be part of a higher history than all history hitherto.' Here the madman fell silent and again regarded his listeners; and they, too, were silent and stared at him in astonishment. At last he threw his lantern to the ground and it broke and went out. 'I come too early,' he said then; 'my time has not yet come. This tremendous event is still on its way, still traveling—it has not yet reached the ears of men. Lightning and thunder require time, deeds require time after they have been done before they can be seen and heard. This deed is still more distant from them than the most distant stars—*and yet they have done it themselves.*'—It has been related further that on that same day the madman entered divers churches and there sang a *requiem aeternam deo.* Led out and quieted, he is said to have retorted each time: 'What are these churches now if they are not the tombs and sepulchers of God?'

[GS 125]

41

The conditions for God.—"God himself cannot exist without wise people," said Luther with good reason. But "God can exist even less without unwise people"—that our good Luther did not say.

[GS 129]

42

[. . .] Let us not be ungrateful to it, even though it certainly has to be admitted that the worst, most wearisomely protracted and most dangerous of all errors hitherto has been a dogmatist's error, namely Plato's invention of pure spirit and the good in itself. [. . .]

[BGE *Preface*]

43

Why atheism today?—'The father' in God is thoroughly refuted; likewise 'the judge', 'the rewarder'. Likewise his 'free will': he does not hear—and if he heard he would still not know how to help. The worst thing is: he seems incapable of making himself clearly understood: is he himself vague about what he means?—These are what, in the course of many conversations, asking and listening, I

found to be the causes of the decline of European theism; it seems to me that the religious instinct is indeed in
vigorous growth—but that it rejects the theistic answer
with profound mistrust.

[BGE 53]

44

[. . .] There are more idols in the world than there are
realities [. . .] That does not prevent their being the *most
believed in* [. . .]

[T *Foreword*]

45

Which is it? Is man only God's mistake or God only
man's mistake?

[T *Maxims and Arrows* 7]

46

You ask me about the idiosyncrasies of philosophers?
. . . There is their lack of historical sense, their hatred of
even the idea of becoming, their Egyptianism. They think
they are doing a thing *honour* when they dehistoricize it,
sub specie aeterni—when they make a mummy of it. All
that philosophers have handled for millennia has been
conceptual mummies; nothing actual has escaped from
their hands alive. They kill, they stuff, when they worship, these conceptual idolaters—they become a mortal
danger to everything when they worship. Death, change,
age, as well as procreation and growth, are for them
objections—refutations even. What is, does not *become*;
what becomes *is* not. . . . Now they all believe, even to
the point of despair, in that which is. But since they cannot get hold of it, they look for reasons why it is being
withheld from them. 'It must be an illusion, a deception

which prevents us from perceiving that which is: where is the deceiver to be found?'—'We've got it,' they cry in delight, 'it is the senses! These senses, *which are so immoral as well*, it is they which deceive us about the real world. Moral: escape from sense-deception, from becoming, from history, from falsehood—history is nothing but belief in the senses, belief in falsehood. Moral: denial of all that believes in the senses, of all the rest of mankind: all of that is mere "people". Be a philosopher, be a mummy, represent monotono-theism by a gravedigger-mimicry!—And away, above all, with the *body*, that pitiable *idée fixe* of the senses! infected with every error of logic there is, refuted, impossible even, notwithstanding it is impudent enough to behave as if it actually existed!' . . .

[T 'Reason' *in Philosophy* 1]

47

[. . .] In so far as the senses show becoming, passing away, change, they do not lie . . . . [. . .] Heraclitus will always be right in this, that being is an empty fiction. The 'apparent' world is the only one: the 'real' world has only been *lyingly added* . . .

[T 'Reason' *in Philosophy* 2]

48

The *other* idiosyncrasy of philosophers is no less perilous: it consists in mistaking the last for the first. They put that which comes at the end—unfortunately! for it ought not to come at all!—the 'highest concepts', that is to say the most general, the emptiest concepts, the last fumes of evaporating reality, at the beginning *as* the beginning. It is again only the expression of their way of doing reverence: the higher must not be *allowed* to grow

out of the lower, must not be *allowed* to have grown at
all . . . .Moral: everything of the first rank must be *causa
sui*. Origin in something else counts as an objection, as
casting a doubt on value. All supreme values are of the
first rank, all the supreme concepts—that which is, the
unconditioned, the good, the true, the perfect—all that
cannot have become, *must* therefore be *causa sui*, But
neither can these supreme concepts be incommensurate
with one another, be incompatible with one another. . . .
Thus they acquired their stupendous concept 'God'. . . .
The last, thinnest, emptiest is placed as the first, as cause
in itelf, as *ens realissimum*. . . . That mankind should
have taken seriously the brain-sick fancies of morbid
cobweb-spinners!—And it has paid dearly for doing so!
. . .

[T 'Reason' *in Philosophy* 4]

49

[. . .] Language belongs in its origin to the age of the
most rudimentary form of psychology: we find ourselves
in the midst of a rude fetishism when we call to mind the
basic presuppositions of the metaphysics of language—which is to say, of *reason*. It is *this* which sees
everywhere deed and doer; this which believes in will as
cause in general; this which believes in the 'ego' [. . .]
and which *projects* its belief in the ego-substance on to
all things—only thus does it *create* the concept 'thing' . .
. . Being is everywhere thought in, *foisted on*, as cause; it
is only from the conception 'ego' that there follows,
derivatively, the concept 'being' [. . .] Very much later, in
a world a thousand times more enlightened, the *security*,
the subjective *certainty* with which the categories of reason could be employed came all of a sudden into
philosophers' heads: they concluded that these could not

have originated in the empirical world—indeed, the entire empirical world was incompatible with them. *Where then do they originate?*—And in India as in Greece they committed the same blunder: 'We must once have dwelt in a higher world'—instead of *in a very much lower one*, which would have been the truth!—'we must have been divine, *for* we possess reason!' [. . .] 'Reason' in language: oh what a deceitful old woman! I fear we are not getting rid of God because we still believe in grammar . . .

[T 'Reason' *in Philosophy* 5]

50

The error of a false causality.—We have always believed we know what a cause is: but whence did we derive our [. . .] belief we possessed this knowledge? From the realm of the celebrated 'inner facts', none of which has up till now been shown to be factual. [. . .] [W]ho would have disputed that a thought is caused? that the ego causes the thought? [. . .] The oldest and longest-lived psychology was at work here [. . .]: every event was to it an action, every action the effect of a will, the world became for it a multiplicity of agents, an agent ('subject') foisted itself upon every event. Man [. . .] derived the concept 'being' only from the concept 'ego', he posited 'things' as possessing being [. . .] according to his concept of the ego as cause. No wonder he later always discovered in things only *that which he had put into them!*—The thing itself, to say it again, the concept 'thing' is merely a reflection of the belief in the ego as cause. [. . .]—To say nothing of the 'thing in itself', that *horrendum pudendum*[1] of the metaphysicians! The error of spirit as cause mistaken for reality! And made the measure of reality! And called *God!*

[T *Four Great Errors* 3]

51

I make war on this theologian instinct: I have found traces of it everywhere. Whoever has theologian blood in his veins has a wrong and dishonest attitude towards all things from the very first. The pathos that develops out of this is called *faith*: closing one's eyes with respect to oneself for good and all so as not to suffer from the sight of incurable falsity. Out of this erroneous perspective on all things one makes a morality, a virtue, a holiness for oneself, one unites the good conscience with seeing *falsely*—one demands that no *other* kind of perspective shall be accorded any value after one has rendered one's own sacrosanct with the names 'God', 'redemption', 'eternity'. I have dug out the theologian instinct everywhere: it is the most widespread, peculiarly *subterranean* form of falsity that exists on earth. What a theologian feels to be true *must* be false: this provides almost a criterion of truth. [. . .]

[A 9]

52

[. . .] the *lie* of a 'moral world-order' permeates the whole evolution even of the most recent philosophy. What does 'moral world-order' mean? That there exists once and for all a will of God as to what man is to do and what he is not to do; that the value of a nation, of an individual is to be measured by how much or how little obedience is accorded the will of God; that the *ruling power* of the will of God, expressed as punishment and reward according to the degree of obedience, is demonstrated in the destiny of a nation, of an individual. [. . .]

[A 26]

53

[. . .] *To overthrow idols* (my word for 'ideals')—that rather is my business. Reality has been deprived of its value, its meaning, its veracity to the same degree as an ideal world has been *fabricated* . . . [. . .]

[EH *Foreword* 2]

54

[. . .] Perhaps I am even envious of Stendahl? He robbed me of the best atheist joke which precisely I could have made: 'God's only excuse is that he does not exist' . . .

[EH *Why I Am So Clever* 3]

55

[. . .] 'where *you* see ideal things, *I* see—human, alas all too human things!' [. . .]

[EH *Human, All Too Human* 1]

---

[1] horrendous obscenity

The Immoralist

The Error of Free Will

56

The fable of intelligible freedom. [. . .] Now one finally discovers that this [human] nature, too, cannot be accountable, in as much as it is altogether a necessary consequence and assembled from the elements and influences of things past and present: that is to say, that man can be made accountable for nothing, not for his nature, nor for his motives, nor for his actions, nor for the effects he produces. One has thereby attained to the knowledge that the history of the moral sensations is the history of an error, the error of accountability, which rests on the error of freedom of will. [. . .] No one is accountable for his deeds, no one for his nature; to judge is the same thing as to be unjust. This applies when the individual judges himself. The proposition is as clear as daylight, and yet here everyone prefers to retreat back into the shadows and untruth: from fear of the consequences.

[HA 39]

57

The innocent element in so-called evil acts.—All 'evil' acts are motivated by the drive to preservation or, more exactly, by the individual's intention of procuring pleasure and avoiding displeasure; so motivated, however, they are not evil. [. . .] The evil acts at which we are now most indignant rest on the error that he who perpetrates them against us possesses free will, that is to say, that he could have *chosen* not to cause us this harm. It is their belief in choice that engenders hatred, revengefulness, deceitfulness, complete degradation of the imagination, while we are far less censorious towards an animal because we regard it as unaccountable. To do injury not from the drive to preservation but as requital—is the consequence of a mistaken judgement and therefore likewise innocent. [. . .]

[HA 99]

58

'Man's actions are always good'.—We do not accuse nature of immorality when it sends us a thunderstorm and makes us wet: why do we call the harmful man immoral? Because in the latter case we assume a voluntarily commanding free-will, in the former necessity. But this distinction is an error. And then: we do not call even intentional harming immoral under all circumstances; one unhesitatingly kills a fly intentionally, for example, merely because one does not like its buzzing, one punishes the criminal intentionally and does him harm so as to protect ourselves and society. [. . .] All morality allows the intentional causing of harm in the case of self-defence: that is, when it is a matter of *self-preservation*. But these two points of view *suffice* to explain all evil

acts perpetrated by men against men: one desires pleasure or to ward off displeasure; it is always in some sense a matter of self-preservation. Socrates and Plato are right: whatever man does he always does the good, that is to say: that which seems to him good (useful) according to the relative degree of his intellect, the measure of his rationality.

[HA 102]

59

Power without victories.—The strongest knowledge (that of the total unfreedom of the human will) is nonetheless the poorest in successes: for it always has the strongest opponent, human vanity.

[AOM 50]

60

The error of free will.—We no longer have any sympathy today with the concept of 'free will': we know only too well what it is—the most infamous of all the arts of the theologian for making mankind 'accountable' in his sense of the word, that is to say for *making mankind dependent on him* . . . I give here only the psychology of making men accountable.—Everywhere accountability is sought, it is usually the instinct for *punishing and judging* which seeks it. One has deprived becoming of its innocence if being in this or that state is traced back to will, to intentions, to accountable acts: the doctrine of will has been invented essentially for the purpose of punishment, that is of *finding guilty.* The whole of the old-style psychology, the psychology of will, has as its precondition the desire of its authors, the priests at the head of the ancient communities, to create for themselves a *right* to ordain punishments—or their desire to

create for God a right to do so . . . . Men were thought of
as 'free' so that they could become *guilty*: consequently,
every action *had* to be thought of as willed, the origin of
every action as lying in the consciousness [. . .] Today,
when we have started to move in the *reverse* direction,
when we immoralists especially are trying with all our
might to remove the concept of guilt and the concept of
punishment from the world and to purge psychology,
history, nature, the social institutions and sanctions of
them, there is in our eyes no more radical opposition
than that of the theologians, who continue to infect the
innocence of becoming with 'punishment' and 'guilt' by
means of the concept of the 'moral world-order'.
Christianity is a hangman's metaphysics . . .

[T *Four Great Errors* 7]

Morality as Anti-Nature

61

Everything has its day.—When man gave all things a sex
he thought, not that he was playing, but that he had
gained a profound insight:—it was only very late that he
confessed to himself what an enormous error this was,
and perhaps even now he has not confessed it completely.—In the same way man has ascribed to all that exists a
connection with morality and laid an *ethical significance*
on the world's back. One day this will have as much
value, and no more, as the belief in the masculinity or
femininity of the sun has today.

[D 3]

62

[. . .] "Just" and "unjust" exist [. . .] only after the institu-
tion of the law. [. . .] To speak of just or unjust *in itself* is
quite senseless; *in itself*, of course, no injury, assault,
exploitation, destruction can be "unjust," since life oper-
ates *essentially*, that is in its basic functions, through
injury, assault, exploitation, destruction and simply cannot be thought of at all without this character. One must
indeed grant something even more unpalatable: that,
from the highest biological standpoint, legal conditions
can never be other than *exceptional conditions*, since
they constitute a partial restriction of the will of life,
which is bent up on power [. . .]

[GM 2.11]

63

[. . .] But why stroke the effeminate ears of our modern
weaklings? Why should *we* give way even one step to
their tartuffery of words? For us psychologists this would
constitute a tartuffery in *deed*, quite apart from the fact
that it would nauseate us. For if a psychologist today has
good taste (others might say, integrity) it consists in resistance to the shamefully *moralized* way of speaking
which has gradually made all modern judgments of men
and things slimy. One should not deceive oneself in this
matter: the most distinctive feature of modern souls and
modern books is not lying but their inveterate *innocence*
in moralistic mendaciousness. To have to rediscover this
"innocence" everywhere—this constitutes perhaps the
most disgusting job among all the precarious tasks a psychologist has to tackle today; [. . .]

[GM 3.19]

64

[. . .] Formerly one made war on passion itself on account of the folly inherent in it: one conspired for its extermination—all the old moral monsters are unanimous that *'il faut tuer les passions'*.[1] The most famous formula for doing this is contained in the New Testament, in the Sermon on the Mount [. . .] There, for example, it is said, with reference to sexuality, 'if thy eye offend thee, pluck it out': fortunately no Christian follows this prescription. To *exterminate* the passions and desires merely in order to do away with their folly and its unpleasant consequences—this itself seems to us today merely an acute form of folly. We no longer admire dentists who *pull out* the teeth to stop them hurting . . . . [. . .] [O]n the soil out of which Christianity grew the concept *'spiritualization* of passion' could not possibly be conceived. For the primitive Church, as is well known, fought *against* the 'intelligent' in favour of the 'poor in spirit': how could one expect from it an intelligent war against passion?—The Church combats the passions with excision in every sense of the word: its practice, its 'cure' is *castration*. It never asks: 'How can one spiritualize, beautify, deify a desire?'—it has at all times laid the emphasis of its discipline on extirpation [. . .]—But to attack the passions at their roots means to attack life at its roots: the practice of the Church is *hostile to life* . . .

[T *Morality as Anti-Nature* 1]

65

—I formulate a principle. All naturalism in morality, that is all *healthy* morality, is dominated by an instinct of life—some commandment of life is fulfilled through a

certain canon of 'shall' and 'shall not', some hindrance
and hostile element on life's road is thereby removed.
Anti-natural morality, that is virtually every morality that
has hitherto been taught, reverenced and preached, turns
on the contrary precisely *against* the instincts of life—it
is a now secret, now loud and impudent *condemnation*
of these instincts. By saying 'God sees into the heart' it
denies the deepest and highest desires of life and takes
God for the *enemy of life* . . . . The saint in whom God
takes pleasure is the ideal castrate . . . . Life is at an end
where the 'kingdom of God' *begins* . . .

[T *Morality as Anti-Nature* 4]

66

One knows my demand of philosophers that they place
themselves *beyond* good and evil—that they have the
illusion of moral judgement *beneath* them. This demand
follows from an insight first formulated by me: *that there
are no moral facts whatever*. Moral judgement has this
in common with religious judgement that it believes in
realities which do not exist. Morality is only an interpretation of certain phenomena, more precisely a *mis*interpretation. Moral judgement belongs, as does religious
judgement, to a level of ignorance at which even the
concept of the real, the distinction between the real and
imaginary, is lacking: so that at such a level 'truth'
denotes nothing but things which we today call 'imagin-
ings'. To this extent moral judgement is never to be taken
literally: as such it never contains anything but nonsense.
But as *semeiotics* it remains of incalculable value: it
reveals, to the informed man at least, the most precious
realities of cultures and inner worlds which did not *know*
enough to 'understand' themselves. Morality is merely

sign-language, merely symptomatology: one must already know *what* it is about to derive profit from it.

[T *The 'Improvers' of Mankind* 1]

67

[. . .] To call the taming of an animal its 'improvement' is in our ears almost a joke. Whoever knows what goes on in menageries is doubtful whether the beasts in them are 'improved'. They are weakened, they are made less harmful, they become *sickly* beasts through the depressive emotion of fear, through pain, through injuries, through hunger.—It is no different with the tamed human being whom the priest has 'improved'. In the early Middle Ages, when the Church was in fact above all a menagerie, one [. . .] 'improved', for example, the noble Teutons. But what did such a Teuton afterwards look like when he had been 'improved' and led into a monastery? Like a caricature of a human being, like an abortion: he had become a 'sinner', he was in a cage, one had imprisoned him behind nothing but sheer terrifying concepts . . . .There he lay now, sick, miserable, filled with ill-will towards himself; full of hatred for the impulses towards life, full of suspicion of all that was still strong and happy. In short, a 'Christian' [. . .]

[T *The 'Improvers' of Mankind* 2]

68

[. . .] I call an animal, a species, an individual depraved when it loses its instincts, when it chooses, when it *prefers* what is harmful to it. A history of the 'higher feelings', of the 'ideals of mankind' [. . .] would almost also constitute an explanation of *why* man is so depraved. I consider life itself instinct for growth, for continuance,

for accumulation of forces, for *power*: where the will
to power is lacking there is decline. My assertion is that
this will is *lacking* in all the supreme values of
mankind—that values of decline, *nihilistic* values hold
sway under the holiest names.

[A 6]

69

My task, to prepare a moment of supreme coming-to-
oneself on the part of mankind, a *great noontide* when it
[. . .] poses the question why? to what end? for the first
time as a *whole*—this task follows of necessity from the
insight that mankind is *not* of itself on the right path, that
it is absolutely *not* divinely directed, that under precisely
its holiest value-concepts rather the instinct of denial, of
decay, the *décadence* instinct has seductively ruled. The
question of the origin of moral values is therefore for me
a question of the *first rank* because it conditions the
future of mankind. The demand that one ought to *believe*
that fundamentally everything is in the best hands, that a
book, the Bible, will set one's mind finally at rest as to
divine governance and wisdom in the destiny of
mankind, is [actually] the will to suppress the truth as to
the pitiable opposite of this, namely that hitherto
mankind has been in the *worst* hands [. . .]. The decisive
sign that reveals the priest (—including the *concealed*
priest, the philosopher) has become master not only
within a certain religious community but in general is
that *décadence* morality [. . .] counts as morality *in itself*,
is the unconditional value everywhere accorded to the
unegoistic and the hostility accorded the egoistic. [. . .]
When within an organism the meanest organ neglects
even to the slightest degree to assert with absolute

certainty its self-preservation, indemnity for its expenditure of force, its 'egoism', the whole degenerates. The physiologist demands *excision* of the degenerate part, he denies any solidarity with it, he is far from pitying it. But the priest *wants* precisely the degeneration of the whole, of mankind: that is why he *conserves* the degenerate part—at this price he dominates mankind . . . What is the purpose of those lying concepts, the *ancillary* concepts of morality 'soul', 'spirit', 'free will', 'God', if it is not the physiological ruination of mankind? . . . When one directs seriousness away from self-preservation, enhancement of bodily strength, when one makes of greensickness an ideal, of contempt for the body 'salvation of the soul', what else is it but a *recipe* for *décadence*? Loss of centre of gravity, resistance to the natural instincts, in a word 'selflessness'—that has hitherto been called *morality* . . .

[EH *Daybreak* 2]

70

I have not been asked [. . .] what the name Zarathustra means in precisely my mouth, in the mouth of the first immoralist: for what constitutes the tremendous uniqueness of that Persian in history is precisely the opposite of this. Zarathustra was the first to see in the struggle between good and evil the actual wheel in the working of things [. . .]. Zarathustra *created* this most fateful of errors, morality: consequently he must also be the first to *recognize* it. [. . .] Have I been understood? The self-overcoming of morality through truthfulness, the self-overcoming of the moralist into his opposite—*into me*—that is what the name Zarathustra means in my mouth.

[EH *Why I Am A Destiny* 3]

71

—But there is also another sense in which I have chosen for myself the word *immoralist* as a mark of distinction and badge of honour [. . .]. No one has yet felt *Christian* morality as *beneath* him: that requires a height, a far-sightedness, a hitherto altogether unheard-of psychological profundity and abysmalness. Christian morality has hitherto been the Circe of all thinkers—they stood in its service. [. . .]

[EH *Why I Am A Destiny* 6]

72

Have I been understood?—What defines me, what sets me apart from all the rest of mankind, is that I have *unmasked* Christian morality. [. . .] It is *not* error as error which horrifies me at the sight of this [. . .]—it is the lack of nature, it is the utterly ghastly fact that *anti-nature* itself has received the highest honours as morality, and has hung over mankind as law, as categorical imperative! . . . To blunder to this extent, *not* as an individual, *not* as a people, but as mankind! . . . That contempt has been taught for the primary instincts of life; that a 'soul', a 'spirit' has been *lyingly invented* in order to destroy the body; that one teaches that there is something unclean in the precondition of life, sexuality; that the evil principle is sought in that which is most profoundly necessary for prosperity, in *strict* selfishness (—the very word is slanderous!); [. . .] *What*! could mankind itself be in *décadence*? [. . .] What is certain is that it has been *taught* only *décadence* values as supreme values. The morality of unselfing is the morality of decline *par excellence* [. . . it] betrays a will to the end, it *denies* the very foundations of life. [. . .]

[EH *Why I Am A Destiny* 7]

73

[. . .] The *unmasking* of Christian morality is an event
without equal, a real catastrophe [. . .]. He who unmasks
morality has therewith unmasked the valuelessness of
all values which are or have been believed in [. . .]. The
concept 'God' invented as the antithetical concept to life
[. . .]. The concept 'the Beyond', 'real world' invented so
as to deprive of value the *only* world which exists—[. . .]
The concept 'soul', 'spirit', finally even 'immortal soul',
invented so as to despise the body, so as to make it
sick—'holy'—so as to bring to all the things in life which
deserve serious attention, the questions of nutriment, res-
idence, cleanliness, weather, a horrifying frivolity! Instead
of health 'salvation of the soul'—which is to say a *folie
circulaire* between spasms of atonement and redemption
hysteria! The concept 'sin' invented together with the
instrument of torture which goes with it, the concept of
'free will', so as to confuse the instincts, so as to make
mistrust of the instincts into second nature! In the concept of the 'selfless', of the 'self-denying' the actual badge
of *décadence*, being *lured* by the harmful, no longer
being *able* to discover where one's advantage lies, self-
destruction, made the sign of value in general, made
'duty', 'holiness', the 'divine' in man! [. . .] And all this
was believed in *as morality*!—*Ecrasez l'infâme!*

[EH *Why I Am A Destiny* 8]

The Absurdity of Altruism

74

Morality as the self-division of man. [. . .] A girl in love
wishes the faithfulness and devotion of her love could be
tested by the faithlessness of the man she loves. A soldier

wishes he could fall on the battlefield for his victorious fatherland: for his supreme desire is victor in the victory of his fatherland. A mother gives to her child that of which she deprives herself, sleep, the best food, if need be her health, her strength.—But are these all unegoistic states? [. . .] Is it not clear that in all these instances man loves *something of himself*, an idea, a desire, an off-spring, more than *something else of himself*, that he thus *divides* his nature and sacrifices one part of it to the other? Is it something *essentially* different from when some obstinate man says: 'I would rather be shot down than move an inch out of that fellow's way'?—The *inclination for something* (wish, impulse, desire) is present in all the above mentioned instances; to give in to it, with all the consequences, is in any event not 'unegoistic'. [. . .]

[HA 57]

75

Fashions in morality.—How the overall moral judge-ments have shifted! The great men of antique morality, Epictetus for instance, knew nothing of the now normal glorification of thinking of others, of living for others; in the light of our moral fashion they would have to be called downright immoral, for they strove with all their might *for* their *ego* and *against* feeling with others (that is to say, with the sufferings and moral frailties of others). Perhaps they would reply to us: 'If you are so boring or ugly an object to yourself, by all means think of others more than of yourself! It is right you should!'

[D 131]

76

To the teachers of selflessness.—A person's virtues are called *good*, not with regard to the effects they produce for him himself, but with regard to the effects we suppose they will produce for us and for society—praise of virtue has always been very little 'selfless', very little 'unegoistic'! For otherwise it must have been seen that virtues (such as industriousness, obedience, chastity, piety, justness) are mostly *injurious* to their possessors, as drives which rule in them too fervently and demandingly and will in no way allow reason to hold them in equilibrium with the other drives. If you possess a virtue, a real whole virtue (and not merely a puny drive towards a virtue!)—you are its *victim*! But that precisely is why your neighbour praises your virtue! [. . .] Praise of the selfless, sacrificing, virtuous—that is to say, of those who do not expend all their strength and reason on *their own* preservation, evolution, elevation, advancement, amplification of their power, but who live modestly and thoughtlessly [. . .] with regard to themselves—this praise is in any event not a product of the spirit of selflessness! One's 'neighbour' praises selflessness because *he derives advantages from it*! [. . .] Herewith is indicated the fundamental contradiction of that morality which is precisely today held in such high esteem: the *motives* for this morality stand in antithesis to its *principle*! That with which this morality wants to prove itself it refutes by its criterion of the moral! [. . .]

[GS 21]

77

[. . .] Even an act performed out of love is supposed to be 'unegoistic'? But you blockheads—! [. . .]

[BGE 220].

78

A criticism of décadence morality.—An 'altruistic' morality, a morality under which egoism *languishes*—is under
all circumstances a bad sign. This applies to individuals,
it applies especially to peoples. The best are lacking
when egoism begins to be lacking. To choose what is
harmful to *oneself*, to be *attracted* by 'disinterested'
motives, almost constitutes the formula for *décadence*.
'Not to seek *one's own* advantage'—that is merely a
moral figleaf for a quite different, namely physiological
fact: 'I no longer know how to *find* my advantage' . . . .
Disgregation of the instincts!—Man is finished when he
becomes altruistic.—Instead of saying simply 'I am no
longer worth anything', the moral lie in the mouth of the
décadent says: 'Nothing is worth anything—*life* is not
worth anything'. [. . .] [T]he vapours of such a poison-tree
jungle sprung up out of putrefaction can poison *life* for
years ahead, for thousands of years ahead . . .

[T *Expeditions of an Untimely Man* 35]

The Folly of Pity

79

To what extent one has to guard against pity.—Pity [. . .]
is a weakness, like every losing of oneself through a
harmful affect. It increases the amount of suffering in the
world: if suffering is here and there indirectly reduced or
removed as a consequence of pity, this occasional and
on the whole insignificant consequence must not be
employed to justify its essential nature, which is, as I
have said, harmful. Supposing it was dominant even for
a single day, mankind would immediately perish of it.

[. . .] He who for a period of time made the experiment of intentionally pursuing occasions for pity in his everyday life and set before his soul all the misery available to him in his surroundings would inevitably grow sick and melancholic. He, however, whose desire it is to serve mankind as a physician *in any sense whatever* will have to be very much on his guard against that sensation—it will paralyze him at every decisive moment and apply a ligature to his knowledge and his subtle helpful hand.

[D 134]

80

[. . .] What was especially at stake was the *value* of the "unegoistic," the instincts of pity, self-abnegation, self-sacrifice [. . .]. But it was against precisely *these* instincts that there spoke from me an ever more fundamental mistrust, an ever more corrosive skepticism! It was precisely here that I saw the *great* danger to mankind, [. . .] the beginning of the end, the dead stop, a retrospective weariness, the will turning *against* life, the tender and sorrowful signs of the ultimate illness: I understood the ever spreading morality of pity that had seized even on philosophers and made them ill, as the most sinister symptom of a European culture that had itself become sinister [. . .]

For this overestimation of and predilection for pity on the part of modern philosophers is something new: hitherto philosophers have been at one as to the *worthlessness* of pity. I name only Plato, Spinoza, La Rochefoucauld and Kant—four spirits as different from one another as possible, but united in one thing: in their low estimation of pity.

[GM *Preface* 5]

81

This problem of the *value* of pity and of the morality of pity [. . .] seems at first to be merely something detached, an isolated question mark; but whoever sticks with it and *learns* how to ask questions here will experience what I experienced—a tremendous new prospect opens up for him, a new possibility comes over him like a vertigo, every kind of mistrust, suspicion, fear leaps up, his belief in morality, in all morality, falters—finally a new demand becomes audible. Let us articulate this *new demand*: we need a *critique* of moral values, *the value of these values themselves must first be called into question*—[. . .] One has taken the *value* of these "values" as given, as factual, as beyond all question; one has hitherto never doubted or hesitated in the slightest degree in supposing 'the good man' to be of greater value than "the evil man," of greater value in the sense of furthering the advancement and prosperity of man in general (the future of man included). But what if the reverse were true? What if a symptom of regression were inherent in the "good," like-wise a danger, a seduction, a poison, a narcotic, through which the present was possibly living *at the expense of the future*? [. . .] So that precisely morality would be to blame if the *highest power and splendor* actually possible to the type man was never in fact attained? So that pre-cisely morality was the danger of dangers?

[GM *Preface* 6]

82

Christianity is called the religion of *pity*.—Pity stands in antithesis to the tonic emotions which enhance the ener-gy of the feeling of life: it has a depressive effect. [. . .]

Suffering itself becomes contagious through pity; sometimes it can bring about a collective loss of life and life-
energy which stands in an absurd relation to the
quantum of its cause (—the case of the death of the
Nazarene). This is the first aspect; but there is an even
more important one. If one judges pity by the value of
the reactions which it usually brings about, its mortally
dangerous character appears in a much clearer light. Pity
on the whole thwarts the law of evolution, which is the
law of *selection*. It preserves what is ripe for destruction;
it defends life's disinherited and condemned; through the
abundance of the ill-constituted of all kinds which it
retains in life it gives life itself a gloomy and questionable aspect. [. . .] To say it again [. . .]: both as a *multipli-
er* of misery and as a *conservator* of everything miserable
it is one of the chief instruments for the advancement of
décadence—pity persuades to *nothingness*! . . . One does
not say 'nothingness': one says 'the Beyond'; or 'God'; or
'*true* life': or Nirvana, redemption, blessedness . . . .This
innocent rhetoric from the domain of religio-moral idiosyncrasy at once appears *much less innocent* when one
grasps *which* tendency is here draping the mantle of sublime words about itself: the tendency *hostile to life*. [. . .]
Nothing in our unhealthy modernity is more unhealthy
than Christian pity. To be physician *here*, to be inexorable *here*, to wield the knife *here*—that pertains to *us*,
that is *our* kind of philanthropy, with that are *we* philosophers, we Hyperboreans![2]—

[A 7]

Morality's Immoral Sources:
Revenge and Ressentiment

83

[. . .] As long as men have existed, man has enjoyed himself too little: that alone, my brothers, is our original sin!

[. . .] Believe me, my friends: stings of conscience teach one to sting.

[Z II *Of the Compassionate*]

84

Revenge on the spirit and other backgrounds of morality.—Morality—where would you think it has its most dangerous and malicious advocates? . . . Here is a man who has turned out a failure [. . .]; such a man poisoned through and through [. . .] falls finally into an habitual condition of revengefulness [. . .] . . . What do you think he needs, absolutely must have, to create for himself in his own eyes the appearance of superiority over more spiritual men, to enjoy, at least in his imagination, the delight of consummate revenge? Always morality, on that you may wager, always the grand moral words, always the thump-thump of justice, wisdom, holiness, virtue, always the stoicism of bearing (—how well stoicism conceals what one does *not* have! . . .), always the cloak of prudent silence, of geniality, of mildness [. . .]

[GS 359 (1887)]

85

[. . .] The knightly-aristocratic value judgements presupposed a powerful physicality, a flourishing, abundant, even overflowing health, together with that which serves to preseve it: war, adventure, hunting, dancing, war games, and in general all that involves vigorous, free, joyful activity. [. . .]

The slave revolt in morality begins when *ressentiment* itself [. . .] gives birth to values: the *ressentiment* of creatures to whom the real reaction, that of the deed, is denied and who can indemnify themselves only through an imaginary revenge. While every noble morality develops from a triumphant affirmation of itself, slave morality from the outset says No to what is 'outside', what is 'different', what is 'not itself': and *this* No is its creative act. This reversal of the value creating view—this *necessary* directing of the eye outwards instead of back to oneself—pertains precisely to *ressentiment*: in order to come into existence, slave morality always first requires a contrary and outer world, it requires, in the language of physiology, an external stimulus in order to act at all—its action is from the very bottom reaction. [. . .] While the noble man lives in trust and openness with himself (*gennaios*, 'nobly born', underlines the nuance 'upright' and probably also 'naive'), the man of *ressentiment* is neither upright nor naive, or honest and straightforward with himself. His soul *squints*: his spirit loves hiding-places, secret paths and back doors, everything covert strikes him as *his* world, *his* security, *his* refreshment; he knows how to keep silent, how not to forget, how to wait, how to make himself provisionally small and humble. [. . .] When the noble man does feel *ressentiment* it consummates and exhausts itself in an immediate reaction, it therefore does not *poison* [. . .] Picture, on the other hand, 'the enemy' as the man of *ressentiment* conceives him—and here precisely is his deed, his creation: he has conceived 'the evil enemy', '*the Evil One*', and this indeed is his basic conception from which he then evolves, as a corresponding and opposing figure, a 'good one'—himself!

This, then, is quite the contrary of what the noble man does, who conceives the basic concept 'good' in advance and spontaneously out of himself and only then creates for himself an idea of 'bad'! This 'bad' of noble origin and that 'evil' out of the cauldron of unsatisfied hatred, [. . .] how different these words 'bad' and 'evil' are, although they are both apparently the opposite of the same concept 'good'. But it is *not* the same concept 'good': one should ask rather precisely *who* is 'evil' in the sense of the morality of *ressentiment*. The answer, in all strictness, is: *precisely* the 'good man' of the other morality, precisely the noble, powerful man, the ruler, but dyed in another color, interpreted in another fashion, seen in another way by the venomous eye of *ressentiment*. [. . .]

Supposing that what is at any rate believed to be the 'truth' really is true, and the *meaning of all culture* is the reduction of the beast of prey 'man' to a tame and civilized animal, a *domestic animal*, then one would undoubtedly have to regard all those instincts of reaction and *ressentiment* through whose aid the noble races and their ideals were finally confounded and overthrown as the actual *instruments of culture*; which is not to say that the *bearers* of these instincts themselves represent culture. Rather is the reverse not merely probable—no! today it is *palpable*! These bearers of the oppressive instincts that thirst for reprisal, the descendants of every kind of European and non-European slavery, [. . .]—they represent the *regression* of mankind! . . .

[GM 1.7, 1.10, 1.11]

86

Would anyone like to take a look into the secret of how *ideals are made* on earth? Who has the courage?—Very well! Here is a point we can see through into this dark workshop. But wait a moment or two, Mr. Rash and Curious: your eyes must first get used to this false iridescent light.—All right! Now speak! What is going on down there? [. . .]

"[. . .] Bad air! Bad air! This workshop where *ideals are manufactured*—it seems to me it stinks of so many lies."

— [. . .] Wait a moment! You have said nothing yet of [. . .] their boldest, subtlest, most ingenious, most mendacious artistic stroke? Attend to them! [. . .]

—"I understand; I'll open my ears again (oh! oh! oh! and *close* my nose). Now I can really hear what they have been saying all along: 'We good men—*we are the just*'—what they desire they call not retaliation, but the triumph of justice'; what they hate is not their enemy, no! they hate 'injustice,' they hate 'godlessness'; what they believe in and hope for is not the hope of revenge, the intoxication of sweet revenge [. . .] but the victory of God, of the *just* God, over the godless; [. . .]"

—And what do they call that which serves to console them for all the suffering of life—their phantasmagoria of anticipated future bliss?

—"What? Do I hear aright? They call that 'the last Judgment,' the coming of *their* kingdom, of the 'Kingdom of God' [. . .]"

[. . .] These weak people—some day or other *they* too intend to be the strong, there is no doubt of that, some day *their* "kingdom" too shall come—they term it "the kingdom of God," of course, as aforesaid: for one is so very humble in all things! To experience *that* one needs to live a long time, beyond death—indeed one needs eternal life, so as to be eternally indemnified in the "kingdom of God" [. . .]

Dante, I think, committed a crude blunder when, with a terror-inspiring ingenuity, he placed above the gateway of his hell the inscription "I too was created by eternal love"—at any rate, there would be more justification for placing above the gateway to the Christian paradise and its "eternal bliss" the inscription "I too was created by eternal *hate*"—provided a truth may be placed above the gateway to a lie! [. . .]

[GM 1.14, 1.15]

87

[. . .] Those who are failures from the start, downtrodden, crushed—it is they, the *weakest*, who must undermine life among men, who call into question and poison most dangerously our trust in life, in man, and in ourselves. Where does one not encounter that [. . .] inward-turned glance of the born failure which betrays how such a man speaks to himself [. . .] "If only I were someone else, [. . .] but there is no hope of that. I am who I am: how could I ever get free of myself? And yet—*I am sick of myself*!"

It is on such soil, on swampy ground, that every weed, every poisonous plant grows, always so small, so hidden, so false, so saccharine. Here the worms of vengefulness and rancor swarm; here the air stinks of secrets and concealment; here the web of the most malicious of all conspiracies is being spun constantly—the conspiracy of the suffering against the well-constituted and victorious, here the aspect of the victorious is *hated*. And what mendaciousness is employed to disguise that this hatred is hatred! What a display of grand words

and postures [. . .] How much sugary, slimy, humble submissiveness swims in their eyes! What do they really
want? At least to *represent* justice, love, wisdom, superiority—that is the ambition of the "lowest," the sick. And
how skillful such an ambition makes them! Admire above
all the forger's skill with which the stamp of virtue, even
the ring, the golden sounding ring of virtue, is here
counterfeited. They monopolize virtue, these weak,
hopelessly sick people, there is no doubt of it: "we alone
are the good and just," they say [. . .] They walk among
us as embodied reproaches [. . .] to us—as if health, well-
constitutedness, strength, pride, and the sense of power
were in themselves necessarily vicious things for which
one must pay some day, and pay bitterly: how ready
they themselves are at bottom to *make* one pay; how
they crave to be *hangmen*. [. . .]—where can it not be
discovered, this will to power of the weakest! [. . .]

They are all men of *ressentiment*, physiologically
unfortunate and worm-eaten, a whole tremulous realm of
subterranean revenge, inexhaustible and insatiable in
outbursts against the fortunate and happy and in masquerades of revenge and pretexts for revenge: when
would they achieve the ultimate, subtlest, sublimest triumph of revenge? Undoubtedly if they succeeded in *poisoning the consciences* of the fortunate with their own
misery, with all misery, so that one day the fortunate
began to be ashamed of their good fortune and perhaps
said one to another: "it is disgraceful to be fortunate:
there is too much misery!"

But no greater or more calamitous misunderstanding
is possible than for the happy, well-constituted, powerful
in soul and body, to begin to doubt their *right to happiness* in this fashion. Away with this "inverted world"!
Away with this shameful emasculation of feeling! [. . .]

And therefore let us have fresh air! fresh air! and
keep clear of the madhouses and hospitals of culture!
And therefore let us have good company, *our* company!
Or solitude, if it must be! But away from the sickening
fumes of inner corruption and the hidden rot of disease!
. . . So that we may, at least for a while yet, guard ourselves, my friends, against the two worst contagions that
may be reserved just for us—against the *great nausea at
man!* against *great pity for man!*

[GM 3.14]

88

The whole labour of the ancient world *in vain* : I have
no words to express my feelings at something so dreadful.—[. . .] Why did the Greeks exist? Why the
Romans?—Every prerequisite for an erudite culture, all
the scientific *methods* were already there, the great, the
incomparable art of reading well had already been established—the prerequisite for a cultural tradition, for a uniform science; natural science, in concert with
mathematics and mechanics, was on the best possible
road—the *sense for facts*, the last-developed and most
valuable of all the senses, had its schools and its tradition
already centuries old! Is this understood? [. . .] Overnight
merely a memory!—Greeks! Romans! [. . .] And not over-
whelmed overnight by a natural event! Not trampled
down by Teutons and other such clodhoppers! But
ruined by cunning, secret, invisible, anaemic vampires!
Not conquered—only sucked dry! . . . Covert revengefulness, petty envy become *master*! Everything pitiful,
everything suffering from itself, everything tormented
by base feelings, the whole *ghetto-world* of the soul suddenly *on top*!—One has only to read any of the Christian

agitators, Saint Augustine for example, to realize, to
smell, what dirty fellows had therewith come out on top.
One would be deceiving oneself utterly if one presupposed a lack of intelligence of any sort on the part of the
leaders of the Christian movement—oh they are shrewd,
shrewd to the point of holiness, these Church Fathers!
What they lack is something quite different. Nature was
neglectful when she made them—she forgot to endow
them with even a modest number of respectable, decent,
cleanly instincts. [. . .]

[A 59]

89

[. . .] the birth of Christianity out of the spirit of *ressentiment, not*, as is no doubt believed, out of the 'spirit'—[is]
essentially a counter-movement, the great revolt against
the domination of *noble* values.

[EH *Genealogy of Morals*]

The Psychology of Guilt

90

The bite of conscience. The bite of conscience, like the
bite of a dog into a stone, is a stupidity.

[WS 38]

91

Guilt.—Although the most clear-sighted judges of witches and even the witches themselves were convinced the
witches were guilty of witchcraft, no guilt in fact existed.
So it is with all guilt.

[GS 250]

92

To breed an animal *with the right to make promises*—is not this the paradoxical task that nature has set itself in the case of man? is it not the real problem regarding man?

That this problem has been solved to a large extent must seem all the more remarkable to anyone who appreciates the strength of the opposing force, that of *forgetfulness*. [. . .] there could be no happiness, no cheerfulness, no hope, no pride, no *present*, without forgetfulness. The man in whom this apparatus of repression is damaged and ceases to function properly may be compared (and more than merely compared) with a dyspeptic—he cannot "have done" with anything.

Now this animal which needs to be forgetful in which forgetting represents a force, a form of *robust* health, has bred in itself an opposing faculty, a memory, with the aid of which forgetfulness is abrogated in certain cases—namely in those cases where promises are made. [. . .] But how many things this presupposes! To ordain the future in advance in this way, man must first have learned to distinguish necessary events from chance ones, to think causally, to see and anticipate distant eventualities as if they belonged to the present, [. . .] and in general be able to calculate and compute. Man himself must first of all have become *calculable, regular, necessary*, even in his own image of himself, if he is to be able to stand security for *his own future*, which is what one who promises does!

This precisely is the long story of how *responsibility* originated. The task of breeding an animal with the right to make promises evidently embraces and presupposes as a preparatory task that one first *makes* men to a

certain degree necessary, uniform, like among like, regular, and consequently calculable. [. . .]

[. . .] "How can one create a memory for the human animal? How can one impress something upon this partly
obtuse, partly flighty mind, attuned only to the passing
moment, in such a way that it will stay there?"

One can well believe that the answers and methods
for solving this primeval problem were not precisely gentle; perhaps indeed there was nothing more fearful and
uncanny in the whole prehistory of man than his
mnemotechnics. "If something is to stay in the memory it
must be burned in: only that which never ceases to *hurt*
stays in the memory"—this is a main clause of the oldest
(unhappily also the most enduring) psychology on earth.
[. . .] Man could never do without blood, torture, and sacrifices when he felt the need to create a memory for himself; the most dreadful sacrifices and pledges (sacrifices
of the first-born among them), the most repulsive mutila-
tions (castration, for example), the cruelest rites of all the
religious cults (and all religions are at the deepest level
systems of cruelties)—all this has its origin in the instinct
that realized that pain is most powerful aid to mnemon-
ics. [. . .]

[GM 2.1-3]

93

[. . .] I regard the bad conscience as the serious illness
which man was bound to contract under the stress of the
most fundamental change he had ever experienced—that
change which occurred when he found himself finally
enclosed within the walls of society and of peace. The
situation that must have faced the sea animals when they
were compelled either to become land animals or perish

was the same as faced these semi-animals which were well adapted to the wilderness, to war, to prowling about, to adventure—suddenly all their instincts were deprived of value and 'suspended'. [. . .] They felt incapable of the simplest undertakings, in this new unfamiliar world their former guides, the regulating and unconsciously certain drives, deserted them—these unhappy creatures were reduced to thinking, inferring, reckoning, co-ordinating cause and effect, to their 'consciousness', to their poorest and most fallible organ! I believe there has never been such a feeling of misery, such leaden discomfort on earth—and at the same time their old instincts had not suddenly ceased to make their demands! Only it was hard and rarely possible to gratify them: as a rule they had to look for new and, as it were, subterranean satisfactions. All instincts which do not discharge themselves outwardly *turn inwards*—this is that which I call the deepening and intensifying [*Verinnerlichung*] of man: thus it was that man first developed what he afterwards called his 'soul'. The entire inner world, originally as thin as if stretched between two membranes, grew and expanded, acquired depth, breadth, height, in the same measure as outward discharge was *hindered*. Those fearful bulwarks with which the social organization protected itself against the old instincts of freedom—punishment is the chief among them—brought it about that all those instincts of wild, free, prowling man turned backwards *against man himself*. [. . .]: *that* is the origin of the 'bad conscience' [. . .] [T]hus was inaugurated the worst and uncanniest illness, from which man has not to the present moment recovered, man's suffering *from man, from himself*: as the consequence of a forcible sundering from his animal past [. . .] Let us add at once that, on the other hand, with the fact of an animal soul turned against itself, taking sides against itself, something so new, profound, unheard-of, enigmatic contradictory *and full of future* was introduced that the aspect of the earth was thereby essentially altered. [. . .] From now on man [. . .] awakens an interest, a tension, a hope, almost a certainty, as if with him something were announcing, preparing itself, as if man were not a goal but only a way, an episode, a bridge, a great promise . . .

[GM 2. 16]

94

[. . .] Guilt before *God*: this thought becomes an instrument of torture [. . .]. He apprehends in "God" the ultimate antithesis of his own ineluctable animal instincts; he reinterprets these animal instincts themselves as a form of guilt before God (as hostility, rebellion, insurrection against the "Lord" [. . .]); he stretches himself upon the contradiction "God" and "Devil"; [. . .]

In this psychical cruelty there resides a madness of the will which is absolutely unexampled: the *will* of man to find himself guilty and reprehensible to a degree that can never be atoned for; [. . .] his *will* to infect and poison the fundamental ground of things with the problem of punishment and guilt so as to cut off once and for all his own exit from this labyrinth of 'fixed ideas'; his *will* to erect an ideal—that of the "holy God"—and in the face of it to feel the palpable certainty of his own absolute unworthiness. Oh this insane, pathetic beast—man! What ideas he has, what unnaturalness, what paroxysms of nonsense, what *bestiality of thought* erupts as soon as he is prevented just a little from being a *beast in deed*!

All this is interesting, to excess, but also of a gloomy, black, unnerving sadness, so that one must forcibly forbid oneself to gaze too long into these abysses. Here is *sickness*, beyond any doubt, the most terrible sickness that has ever raged in man; [. . .] —Too long, the earth has been a madhouse!

[GM 2.22]

95

[. . .] The chief trick the ascetic priest permitted himself [. . .] was, as everyone knows, the exploitation of the *sense of guilt*. [. . .] It was only in the hands of the priest, that artist in guilt feelings, that it achieved form—oh, what a form! "Sin"—for this is the priestly name for the animal's "bad conscience" [. . .]—has been the greatest event so far in the history of the sick soul [. . .]. Man, suffering from himself [. . .], thirsting for reasons [. . .], receives from [. . .] the ascetic priest, the *first* hint as to the "cause" of his suffering: he must seek it in *himself*, in some *guilt*, in a piece of the past, he must understand his suffering as a *punishment*.[. . .]

For two millennia now we have been condemned to the sight of this new type of invalid, 'the sinner'—shall it always be so?—[. . .] [T]he ascetic priest—he had obviously won, *his* kingdom had come: one no longer protested *against* pain, one *thirsted* for pain; '*more* pain! *more* pain!' the desire of his disciples and initiates has cried for centuries. Every painful orgy of feeling, [. . .] the secrets of the torture chamber, the inventiveness of hell itself—[. . .] all served henceforward to promote the victory of his ideal, the ascetic ideal.—"My kingdom is not of *this* world"—he continued to say, as before: but did he still have the right to say it?

[GM 3.20]

96

[. . .] the psychology of the *conscience*: it is *not*, as is no doubt believed, 'the voice of God in man'—it is the instinct of cruelty turned backwards after it can no longer discharge itself outwards. Cruelty [is] here brought to light for the first time as one of the oldest substrata of culture and one that can least be thought away. [. . .]

[EH *Genealogy of Morals*]

Herd-Morality and the Lie of Equality

97

Herd instinct.—Where we encounter a morality we find a valuation and order of rank of human drives and actions. These valuations and orders of rank are always the expression of the needs of a community and herd [. . .] With morality the individual is led into being a function of the herd [. . .] Morality is the herd instinct in the individual.

[GS 116]

98

[. . .] I do not want to be confused with these preachers of equality, nor taken for one of them. For justice speaks thus *to me*: 'Men are not equal.' [. . .]

[Z II *Of the Tarantulas*]

99

[. . .] Christianity has been the most fatal kind of self-presumption ever. Men not high or hard enough for the artistic refashioning of *mankind*; men not strong or farsighted enough for the sublime self-constraint needed to *allow* the foreground law of thousandfold failure and

perishing to prevail; men not noble enough to see the
abysmal disparity in order of rank and abysm of rank
between man and man—it is *such* men who, with their
'equal before God', have hitherto ruled over the destiny
of Europe, until at last a shrunken, almost ludicrous
species, a herd animal, something full of good will, sickly
and mediocre has been bred, the European of today . . .

[BGE 62]

100

Madness is something rare in individuals—but in groups,
parties, peoples, ages it is the rule.

[BGE 156]

101

[. . .] Moralities must [. . .] come to understand that it is
immoral to say: 'What is good for one is good for another.' [. . .]

[BGE 221]

102

[. . .] the judgement 'good' does *not* originate with those
to whom 'goodness' is shown! It was rather 'the good'
themselves, that is to say the noble, powerful, higher
placed and high-minded, who felt and posited themselves and their actions as good, namely as of the first
rank, in antithesis to everything low, low-minded, common and plebeian. It was out of this *pathos of distance*
that they assumed the right to create values, to coin the
names of values [. . .] The pathos of nobility and distance, [. . .] the permanent and domineering collective
fundamental feeling of a higher ruling type in relation
to a lower type, to a 'beneath'—*that* is the origin of
the antithesis 'good' and 'bad'. [. . .] It is because of this

origin that the word 'good' was from the very first absolutely *not* necessarily connected with 'unegoistic' actions [. . .] It is rather only with a *decline* in aristocratic value judgements that this whole antithesis 'egoistic' 'unegoistic' obtrudes itself more and more on the human conscience—it is, to employ my own language, *the herd instinct* which with this antithesis at length finds speech (and words to speak with). [. . .]

The signpost to the *right* track [to the discovery of the origin of the value judgement 'good'] was the question: what was the real etymological significance of the symbols for 'good' which have been coined in the various languages? I found they all led back to the *same conceptual transformation*—that everywhere 'noble', 'aristocratic' in the social sense is the basic concept from which 'good' in the sense of 'with aristocratic soul', 'noble', 'with a soul of a higher order', 'with a privileged soul' necessarily developed: a development which always runs parallel with that other in which 'common', 'plebian', 'low', are finally transformed into the concept 'bad'. The most convincing instance of the latter is the German word *schlecht* [bad] itself: which is identical with *schlicht* [plain] [. . .] and originally designated the plain, common man, as yet without any inculpatory side-glance but simply in antithesis to the nobleman. About the time of the Thirty Years War—recently enough, that is—this sense shifted to the one now current.—With respect to the genealogy of morals this seems to me an essential insight: that it was arrived at only so late is to be attributed to the retarding influence exercised by the democratic prejudice within the modern world in regard to all questions of origin. [. . .]

[GM 1.2, 1.4]

103

[. . .] the strong are as naturally inclined to *separate* as the weak are to *congregate* [. . .]

[GM 3.18]

104

My conception of freedom.—The value of a thing sometimes lies not in what one attains with it, but in what one pays for it—what it *costs* us. I give an example. Liberal institutions immediately cease to be liberal as soon as they are attained: subsequently there is nothing more thoroughly harmful to freedom than liberal institutions. One knows, indeed, *what* they bring about: they undermine the will to power, they are the levelling of mountain and valley exalted to a moral principle, they make small, cowardly and smug—it is the herd animal which triumphs with them every time. Liberalism: in plain words, *reduction to the herd animal*. . . . [. . .]

[T *Expeditions of an Untimely Man* 38]

105

[. . .] The bloody farce enacted by this [French] Revolution [. . .] does not concern me much: what I hate is its Rousseauesque *morality*—the so-called 'truths' of the Revolution through which it is still an active force and persuades everything shallow and mediocre over to its side. The doctrine of equality! . . . But there exists no more poisonous poison: for it *seems* to be preached by justice itself, while it is the *end* of justice. . . . 'Equality for equals, inequality for unequals'—*that* would be the true voice of justice: and, what follows from it, 'Never make equal what is unequal'. [. . .]

[T *Expeditions of an Untimely Man* 48]

---

[1] It is necessary to kill the passions

[2] In Greek mythology, those who dwell beyond (hyper) Boreas (the north wind) in a paradise of warmth, health and plenty.

Against Christianity

The Good News of Jesus

106

In the entire psychology of the 'Gospel' the concept guilt and punishment is lacking; likewise the concept reward. 'Sin', every kind of distancing relationship between God and man, is abolished—*precisely this is the 'glad tidings'*. Blessedness is not promised, it is not tied to any conditions: it is the *only* reality—the rest is signs for speaking of it . . .

The *consequence* of such a condition projects itself into a new *practice*, the true evangelic practice. It is not a 'belief' which distinguishes the Christian: the Christian acts, he is distinguished by a *different* mode of acting. Neither by words nor in his heart does he resist the man who does him evil. He makes no distinction between foreigner and native, between Jew and non-Jew [. . .].

The life of the redeemer was nothing else than *this* practice—his death too was nothing else. . . . He no longer required any formulas, any rites for communicating with God—not even prayer. He has settled his

accounts with the whole Jewish penance-and-reconcilia-
tion doctrine; he knows that it is through the *practice* of
one's life that one feels 'divine', 'blessed', 'evangelic', at
all times a 'child of God'. It is *not* 'penance', *not* 'prayer
for forgiveness' which leads to God: *evangelic practice
alone* leads to God, it *is* God!—What was *abolished* with
the Evangel was the Judaism of the concepts 'sin', 'forgiveness of sin', 'faith', 'redemption by faith'—the whole
of Jewish *ecclesiastical* teaching was denied in the 'glad
tidings'.

The profound instinct for how one would have to
live in order to feel oneself 'in Heaven', to feel oneself
'eternal', while in every other condition one by *no* means
feels oneself 'in Heaven': this alone is the psychological
reality of 'redemption'.—A new way of living, *not* a new
belief . . .

[A 33]

107

If I understand anything of this great symbolist it is that
he took for realities, for 'truths', only *inner* realities—that
he understood the rest, everything pertaining to nature,
time, space, history, only as signs, as occasion for
metaphor. The concept 'the Son of Man' is not a concrete
person belonging to history, anything at all individual or
unique, but an 'eternal' fact, a psychological symbol
freed from the time concept. The same applies supreme-
ly to the *God* of this typical symbolist, to the 'kingdom of
God', to the 'kingdom of Heaven', to 'God's children'.
Nothing is more un-Christian than the *ecclesiastical cru-
dities* of a God as a *person*, of a 'kingdom of God' which
comes, of a 'kingdom of Heaven' in the *Beyond*, of a 'Son
of God', the *second person* of the Trinity. All this—forgive
the expression—a *fist* in the eye[1]—oh in what an

eye!—of the Gospel: *world-historical cynicism* in the mockery of symbolism. . . . But it is patently obvious what is alluded to in the symbols 'Father' and 'Son'—not patently obvious to everyone, I grant: in the word 'Son' is expressed the *entry* into the collective feeling of the transfiguration of all things (blessedness), in the word 'Father' *this feeling itself*, the feeling of perfection and eternity. [. . .]

The 'kingdom of Heaven' is a condition of the heart—not something that comes 'upon the earth' or 'after death'. [. . .] The 'kingdom of God' is not something one waits for; it has no yesterday or tomorrow, it does not come 'in a thousand years'—it is an experience within a heart; it is everywhere, it is nowhere . . .

[A 34]

108

This 'bringer of glad tidings' died as he lived, as he *taught*—*not* to 'redeem mankind' but to demonstrate how one ought to live. What he bequeathed to mankind is his *practice*: his bearing before the judges, before the guards, before the accusers and every kind of calumny and mockery—his bearing on the *Cross*. [. . .] And he entreats, he suffers, he loves *with* those, *in* those who are doing evil to him. His words to the *thief* on the Cross contain the whole Evangel. 'That was verily a *divine* man, a child of God!'—says the thief. 'If thou feelest this'—answers the redeemer—*'thou art in Paradise*, thou art a child of God.' *Not* to defend oneself, *not* to grow angry, *not* to make responsible. . . .But not to resist even the evil man—to *love* him . . .

[A 35]

109

[. . .] in reality there has been only one Christian, and he died on the Cross.

[A 39]

Good News Gone Bad:
Christianity's Betrayal of Jesus

110

The persecutor of God. Paul thought up the idea, and Calvin re-thought it, that for innumerable people damnation has been decreed from eternity, and that this beautiful world plan was instituted to reveal the glory of God: heaven and hell and humanity are thus supposed to exist—to satisfy the vanity of God! What cruel and insatiable vanity must have flared in the soul of the man who thought this up first, or second. Paul has remained Saul after all—the persecutor of God.

[WS 85]

111

—Our age is proud of its historical sense: how was it able to make itself believe in the nonsensical notion that the *crude miracle-worker and redeemer fable* comes at the commencement of Christianity—and that everything spiritual and symbolic is only a subsequent development? On the contrary: the history of Christianity—and that from the very death on the Cross—is the history of progressively cruder misunderstanding of an *original* symbolism. With every extension of Christianity over even broader, even ruder masses in whom the preconditions out of which it was born were more and more lacking, it

became increasingly necessary to *vulgarize*, to *barbarize*
Christianity—it absorbed the doctrines and rites of every
subterranean cult of the *Imperium Romanum*, it
absorbed the absurdities of every sort of morbid reason.
[. . .]

[A 37]

112

[. . .] I shall now relate the *real* history of Christianity.
[. . .] What was called 'Evangel' from this moment
onwards was already the opposite of what *he* had lived:
'*bad* tidings', a *dysangel*. It is false to the point of absurdity to see in a 'belief'[. . .] the distinguishing characteristic of the Christian: only Christian *practice*, a life such as
he who died on the Cross *lived*, is Christian. . . . Even
today *such* a life is possible, for *certain* men even necessary: genuine, primitive Christianity will be possible at all
times . . . . *Not* a belief but a doing, above all a *not*-doing
of many things, a different *being*. . . . [. . .] To reduce
being a Christian, Christianness, to a holding something
to be true, to a mere phenomenality of consciousness,
means to negate Christianness. [. . .]

[A 39]

113

[. . .] It was only [. . .] this unexpected shameful death,
only the Cross, which [. . .] brought the disciples face to
face with the real enigma: '*Who was that? What was
that?*'—The feeling of being shaken and disappointed to
their depths, the suspicion that such a death might be the
refutation of their cause [. . .]—this condition is only too
understandable. Here everything *had* to be necessary,
meaningful, reasonable, reasonable in the highest

degree; a disciple's love knows nothing of chance. Only
now did the chasm open up: '*Who* killed him? *who* was
his natural enemy?'—this question came like a flash of
lightning. Answer: *ruling* Judaism, its upper class. From
this moment one felt oneself in mutiny *against* the social
order, one subsequently understood Jesus as having been
in mutiny against the social order. Up till then this warlike trait, this negative trait in word and deed, was *lacking* in his image; more, he was the contradiction of it.
Clearly the little community had *failed* to understand precisely the main thing, the exemplary element in his man-
ner of dying, the freedom from, the superiority *over*
every feeling of *ressentiment*:—a sign of how little they
understood of him at all! Jesus himself could have
desired nothing by his death but publicly to offer the
sternest test, the *proof* of his teaching. . . . But his disciples were far from *forgiving* his death—which would
have been evangelic in the highest sense; [. . .] Precisely
the most unevangelic of feelings, *revengefulness*, again
came uppermost. The affair could not possibly be at an
end with this death: one required 'retribution', 'judgement' (—and yet what can be more unevangelic than
'retribution', 'punishment', 'sitting in judgement'!). The
popular expectation of a Messiah came once more into
the foreground; an historic moment appeared in view:
the 'kingdom of God' is coming to sit in judgement on its
enemies. . . . But with this everything is misunderstood:
the 'kingdom of God' as a last act, as a promise! For the
Evangel had been precisely the existence, the fulfilment,
the *actuality* of this 'kingdom'. Such a death *was* precisely this 'kingdom of God'. [. . .]

[A 40]

114

—And now an absurd problem came up: 'How *could* God have permitted that?' For this question the deranged reason of the little community found a downright terrifyingly absurd answer: God gave his Son for the forgiveness of sins, as a *sacrifice*. All at once it was all over with the Gospel! The *guilt sacrifice*, and that in its most repulsive, barbaric form, the sacrifice of the *innocent man* for the sins of the guilty! What atrocious paganism!—For Jesus had done away with the concept 'guilt' itself—he had denied any chasm between God and man, he *lived* this unity of God and man as *his* 'glad tidings'. . . . And *not* as a special prerogative!—From now on there is introduced into the type of the redeemer step by step: the doctrine of a Judgement and a Second Coming, the doctrine of his death as a sacrificial death, the doctrine of the Resurrection with which the entire concept 'blessedness', the whole and sole reality of the Evangel, is juggled away—for the benefit of a state *after* death! . . . Paul [. . .] rationalized this interpretation, this *indecency* of an interpretation, thus: '*If* Christ is not resurrected from the dead our faith is vain'.—All at once the Evangel became the most contemptible of all unfulfillable promises, the *impudent* doctrine of personal immortality. [. . .]

[A 41]

115

[. . .] On the heels of the 'glad tidings' came the *worst of all*: those of Paul.[2] In Paul was embodied the antithetical type to the 'bringer of glad tidings', the genius of hatred, of the vision of hatred, of the inexorable logic of hatred. *What* did this dysangelist not sacrifice to his hatred! The redeemer above all: he nailed him to *his* Cross. The life, the example, the teaching, the death, the meaning and the right of the entire Gospel—nothing was left once this hate-obsessed false-coiner had grasped what alone he could make use of. *Not* the reality, *not* the historical truth! [. . .] Paul simply shifted the centre of gravity of that entire existence *beyond* this existence—in the *lie* of the 'resurrected' Jesus. In fact he could make no use at all of the redeemer's life—he needed the death on the Cross *and* something in addition. . . . To regard as honest a Paul [. . .] when he makes of a hallucination the *proof* that the redeemer is *still* living, or even to believe his story that he had this hallucination, would be a real *niaiserie* on the part of a psychologist: Paul willed the end, *consequently* he willed the means. . . .What he himself did not believe was believed by the idiots among whom he cast *his* teaching.—*His* requirement was *power*; with Paul the priest again sought power—he could employ only those concepts, teachings, symbols with which one tyrannizes over masses, forms herds. *What* was the only thing Mohammed later borrowed from Christianity? The invention of Paul, his means for establishing a priestly tyranny, for forming herds: the belief in immortality—*that is to say the doctrine of 'judgement'* . . .

[A 42]

Why Nietzsche is Not a Christian

116

Destiny of Christianity.—Christianity came into existence in order to lighten the heart; but now it has first to burden the heart so as afterwards to be able to lighten it. Consequently it will perish.

[HA 119]

117

On the Christian need of redemption.—Careful reflection ought to be able to yield an explanation of the occurrence in the soul of a Christian called need of redemption which is free of mythology; that is to say, a purely psychological explanation. [. . .] Man is conscious of certain actions which stand low in the customary order of rank of actions; indeed he discovers in himself a tendency to actions of this sort [. . .] How much he would like to attempt that other species of actions which in the general estimation are accounted the highest, how much he would like to feel full of that good consciousness which is supposed to attend a selfless mode of thought! Unhappily he gets no further than desiring this: his discontent at his insufficiency is added to all the other kinds of discontent [. . .] in him; so that there arises a profound depression of spirits, together with a watching-out for a physician who might be able to alleviate this condition and all its causes.—This condition would not be felt so bitterly if man compared himself only with other men for then he would have no reason to be especially discontented with himself [. . .]. But he compares himself with a being which alone is capable of those actions called unegoistic [. . .], with God; it is because he looks into this brilliant mirror that his own nature seems to him so dismal, so uncommonly distorted. [. . .]

[. . .] [L]et us confess to ourselves that the man in this condition has got into it, not through his 'guilt' and 'sin', but through a succession of errors of reason, that it was the fault of the mirror if his nature appeared to him dark and hateful to such a degree, and that this mirror was *his* work, the very imperfect work of human imagination and judgement. [. . .] The Christian who compares his nature with that of God is like Don Quixote, who underestimated his own courage because his head was filled with the miraculous deeds of the heroes of chivalric romances: the standard of comparison applied in both cases belongs in the domain of fable. [. . .]

Now if [. . .] the Christian has got into the feeling of self-contempt through certain errors [. . .], he also notices with the highest astonishment that this condition of contempt, the pang of conscience [. . .], does not persist, but that occasionally there are hours when all this is wafted away from his soul and he again feels free and valiant. What has happened is that his pleasure in himself, his contentment at his own strength, has [. . .] carried off the victory: he loves himself again, he feels it—but precisely this love, this new self-valuation seems to him incredible, he can see in it only the wholly undeserved flowing down of a radiance of mercy from on high. If he earlier believed he saw in every event warnings, menaces, punishments and every sort of sign of divine wrath, he now *interprets* divine goodness *into* his experiences [. . .]; he conceives his mood of consolation as the effect upon him of an external power, the love with which fundamentally he loves himself appears as divine love; [. . .]

Thus: a definite false psychology, a certain kind of fantasy in the interpretation of motives and experiences is the necessary presupposition for becoming a Christian and for feeling the need of redemption. With the insight into this aberration of reason and imagination one ceases to be a Christian.

[HA 132–135]

118

'*Love.*'—The subtlest artifice which Christianity has over the other religions is a word: it spoke of *love*. [. . .] There

is in the word love something so ambiguous and sugges-
tive, something which speaks to the memory and to
future hope, that even the meanest intelligence and the
coldest heart still feels something of the lustre of this
word. The shrewdest woman and the commonest man
think when they hear it of the relatively least selfish
moments of their whole life, even if Eros has only paid
them a passing visit; and those countless numbers who
never experience love [. . .] have made their find in
Christianity.

[AOM 95]

119

To think a thing evil means to make it evil.—The passions
become evil and malicious if they are regarded as evil
and malicious. Thus Christianity has succeeded in transforming Eros and Aphrodite [. . .] into diabolical kobolds
[. . .] by means of the torments it introduces into the consciences of believers whenever they are excited sexually.
Is it not dreadful to make necessary and regularly recur-
ring sensations into a source of inner misery [. . .]! And
ought one to call Eros an enemy? The sexual sensations
have this in common with the sensations of sympathy
and worship, that one person, by doing what pleases
him, gives pleasure to another person—such benvolent
arrangements are not to be found so very often in nature!
And to calumniate such an arrangement and to ruin it
through associating it with a bad conscience!—In the end
this *diabolising* of Eros aquired an outcome in comedy:
thanks to the dark secretiveness of the church in all
things erotic, the 'devil' Eros gradually became more
interesting to mankind than all the saints and angels put
together: the effect has been that, to this very day, the

love story is the only thing which *all* circles find equally interesting—and with an exaggeratedness which antiquity would have found incomprehensible and which will one day again elicit laughter. All our thinking and poetising, from the highest to the lowest, is characterised, and more than characterised, by the excessive importance attached to the love story: on this account it may be that posterity will judge the whole inheritance of Christian culture to be marked by something crackbrained and petty.

[D 76]

120

The philology of Christianity.—How little Christianity educates the sense of honesty and justice can be gauged fairly well from the character of its scholars' writings: they present their conjectures as boldly as if they were dogmas and are rarely in any honest perplexity over the interpretation of a passage in the Bible. Again and again they say, 'I am right, for it is written—' and then follows an interpretation of such impudent arbitrariness that a philologist who hears it is caught between rage and laughter and asks himself: is it possible? Is this honorable? Is it even decent?—How much dishonesty in this matter is still practiced in Protestant pulpits, how grossly the preacher exploits the advantage that no one is going to interrupt him here, how the Bible is pummelled and punched and the *art of reading badly* is in all due form imparted to the people: only he who never goes to church or never goes anywhere else will underestimate that. [. . .]

[D 84]

121

In Christianity neither morality nor religion come into contact with reality at any point. Nothing but imaginary *causes* ('God', 'soul', 'ego', 'spirit', 'free will' [. . .]): nothing but imaginary *effects* ('sin', 'redemption', 'grace', 'punishment', 'forgiveness of sins'). A traffic between imaginary *beings* ('God', 'spirits', 'souls'); [. . .] an imaginary *psychology* (nothing but self-misunderstandings, interpretations of pleasant or unpleasant general feelings [. . .] an imaginary *teleology* ('the kingdom of God', 'the Last Judgement', 'eternal life') [. . .] Once the concept 'nature' had been devised as the concept antithetical to 'God', 'natural' had to be the word for 'reprehensible'—this entire fictional world has its roots in *hatred* of the natural (—actuality!—), it is the expression of a profound discontent with the actual. [. . .]

[A 15]

122

The Christian conception of God [. . .] is one of the most corrupt conceptions of God arrived at on earth: [. . .] God degenerated to the *contradiction of life*, instead of being its transfiguration and eternal *Yes!* In God a declaration of hostility towards life, nature, the will to life! God the formula for every calumny of 'this world', for every lie about 'the next world'! In God nothingness deified, the will to nothingness sanctified! . . .

[A 18]

123

[. . .] Christianity [. . .] knows that it is in itself a matter of absolute indifference whether a thing be true, but a

matter of the highest importance to *what extent* it is
believed to be true. [. . .] If [. . .] there is *happiness* to be
found in believing oneself redeemed from sin, it is *not*
necessary for a man first to be sinful, but for him to *feel*
himself sinful. If, however, it is *belief* as such which is
necessary above all else, then one has to bring reason,
knowledge, inquiry into disrepute: the road to truth
becomes the *forbidden* road.—Intense *hope* is a much
stronger stimulant to life than any single instance of happiness which actually occurs. Sufferers have to be sustained by a hope which cannot be refuted by any
actuality [. . .]: a hope in the Beyond. [. . .]—So that *love*
shall be possible, God has to be a person [. . .]. Love is
the state in which man sees things most of all as they are
not. The illusion-creating force is there at its height, likewise the sweetening and *transforming* force. One
endures more when in love than one otherwise would,
one tolerates everything. [. . .] —So much for the three
Christian virtues faith, hope and charity: I call them the
three Christian *shrewdnesses*. [. . .]

[A 23]

124

[. . .] Disobedience of God, that is to say of the priest, of
'the Law', now acquires the name 'sin' [. . .]. From a psychological point of view, 'sins' are indispensable in any
society organized by priests: they are the actual levers of
power, the priest *lives* on sins, he needs 'the commission
of sins'. [. . .]

[A 26]

125

—At this point I shall not suppress a sigh. There are days
when I am haunted by a feeling blacker than the blackest

melancholy—*contempt of man*. [. . .] With regard to the past I am, like all men of knowledge, of a large tolerance, that is to say a *magnanimous* self-control: I traverse the madhouse-world of entire millennia, be it called 'Christianity', 'Christian faith', 'Christian Church', with a gloomy circumspection—I take care not to make mankind responsible for its insanities. But my feelings suddenly alter, burst forth, [when] I enter the modern age, our age. [. . .] What was formerly merely morbid has today become indecent—it is indecent to be a Christian today. [. . .] Even with the most modest claim to integrity one *must* know today that a theologian [. . .] does not merely err in every sentence he speaks, he *lies*—that he is no longer free to lie 'innocently', out of 'ignorance'. The priest knows as well as anyone that there is no longer any 'God', any 'sinner', any 'redeemer'—that 'free will', 'moral world-order' are lies—intellectual seriousness, the profound self-overcoming of the intellect, no longer *permits* anyone *not* to know about these things. [. . .]—the concepts 'Beyond', 'Last Judgement', 'immortality of the soul', the 'soul' itself: they are instruments [. . .] by virtue of which the priest has become master, stays master . . . .Everyone know this: *and everyone nonetheless remains unchanged*.

[A 38]

126

If one shifts the centre of gravity of life *out* of life into the 'Beyond'—into *nothingness*—one has deprived life as such of its centre of gravity. The great lie of personal immortality destroys all rationality, all naturalness of instinct—all that is salutary, all that is life-furthering [. . .] excites mistrust. [. . .] That, as an 'immortal soul', everybody is equal to everybody else, that in the totality of beings the 'salvation' of *every* single one is permitted to claim to be of everlasting moment, that little bigots and three-quarters madmen are permitted to imagine that for their sakes the laws of nature are continually being *broken*—such a raising of every sort of egoism to infinity, to *impudence*, cannot be branded with sufficient contempt. And yet it is to *this* pitiable flattery of personal vanity that Christianity owes its *victory* [. . .]. 'Salvation of the soul'—in plain words: 'The world revolves around *me*'. [. . .]

[A 43]

127

[. . .] One must not let oneself be misled: they say 'Judge not!' but they send to Hell everything that stands in their way. [. . .] The reality is that here the most conscious *arrogance of the elect* is posing as modesty: one has placed *oneself*, the 'community', the 'good and just', once and for all on one side, on the side of 'truth'—and the rest, 'the world', on the other. . . . That has been the most fateful kind of megalomania that has ever existed on earth: little abortions of bigots and liars began to lay claim to the concepts 'God', 'truth', 'light', 'spirit', 'love', 'wisdom', 'life' as if these were synonyms of themselves [. . .]

[A 44]

128

—I give a few examples of what these petty people have taken into their heads, what they have put into the mouth of their Master: [. . .]—

    'And whosoever shall not receive you, nor hear you, when ye depart thence, shake the dust off your feet for a testimony against them. Verily I say unto you, It shall be

more tolerable for Sodom and Gomorrah in the day of
judgement, than for that city.' (Mark vi, 11)—How evangelic! . . .

'And whosoever shall offend one of these little ones
that believe in me, it is better for him that a millstone
were hanged about his neck, and he were cast into the
sea.' (Mark ix, 42)—How evangelic! . . . [. . .]

'For if ye love them which love you, *what reward
have ye*? do not even the publicans do the same? [. . .]
(Matthew v, 46–7)—Principle of 'Christian love': it wants
to be well *paid* . . .

'But if ye forgive not men their trespasses, neither
will your Father forgive your trespasses.' (Matthew vi,
15)—Very compromising for the said 'Father' . . . [. . .]

[A 45]

129

What sets *us* apart is not that we recognize no God,
either in history or in nature or behind nature—but that
we find that which has been reverenced as God not
'godlike' but pitiable, absurd, harmful, not merely an
error, but a *crime against life*. [. . .] If this God of the
Christians were proved to us to exist, we should know
even less how to believe in him.—In a formula: *Deus,
qualem Paulus creavit, dei negatio*.[3] [. . .]

[A 47]

130

—With that I have done and pronounce my judgement. I
condemn Christianity, I bring against the Christian
Church the most terrible charge any prosecutor has ever
uttered. To me it is the extremest thinkable form of corruption [. . .]. The Christian Church has left nothing
untouched by its depravity, it has made of every value a

disvalue, of every truth a lie, of every kind of integrity a vileness of soul. People still dare to talk to me of its 'humanitarian' blessings! To *abolish* any state of distress whatever has been profoundly inexpedient to it: it has lived on states of distress, it has *created* states of distress in order to eternalize *itself*. . . . The worm of sin, for example: it was only the Church which enriched mankind with this state of distress!—[. . .] 'Humanitarian' blessings of Christianity! To cultivate out of *humanitas* a self-contradiction, an art of self-violation, a will to false-hood at any price, an antipathy, a contempt for every good and honest instinct! These are the blessings of Christianity!—Parasitism as the *sole* practice of the Church; with its ideal of green-sickness, of 'holiness' draining away all blood, all love, all hope for life; the Beyond as the will to deny reality of every kind; the Cross as the badge of recognition for the most subterranean conspiracy there has ever been—a conspiracy against health, beauty, well-constitutedness, bravery, intellect, *benevolence* of soul, *against life itself* . . .

Wherever there are walls I shall inscribe this eternal accusation against Christianity upon them—I can write in letters which make even the blind see. . . . call Christianity the *one* great curse, the *one* great intrinsic depravity, the *one* great instinct for revenge for which no expedient is sufficiently poisonous, secret, subterranean, *petty*—I call it the *one* immortal blemish of mankind . . .

And one calculates *time* [. . .] from the *first* day of Christianity!—*Why not rather from its last* ?—*From today* ? —Revaluation of all values!

[A 62]

---

[1] A German idiom meaning a complete unlikeness between two things

[2] The reader who wishes to hear more of Nietzsche's assessment of Paul is referred to *Daybreak*, Section 68

[3] God, as Paul created him, is a denial of God

The Creator

Behold the faithful of all faiths! Whom do they hate the most? Him who smashes their tables of values, the breaker, the law-breaker—but he is the creator.

The creator seeks companions, not corpses of herds or believers. The creator seeks fellow-creators, those who inscribe new values on new tables.

[Z I *Prologue* 9]

Do you call yourself free? I want to hear your ruling idea, and not that you have escaped from a yoke. [. . .]

Free from what? Zarathustra does not care about that! But your eye should clearly tell me: free *for* what?

[Z I *Of the Way of the Creator*]

I [. . .] am none the less the opposite of a negative spirit. I am a *bringer of good tidings* such as there has never been [. . .]

[EH *Why I Am A Destiny* 1]

The Free Spirit

The Open Sea

Unaccountability and innocence.—The complete unaccountability of man for his actions and his nature is the bitterest draught the man of knowledge has to swallow if he has been accustomed to seeing in accountability and duty the patent of his humanity. All his evaluations [. . .] rested upon an error; he may no longer praise, no longer censure, for it is absurd to praise and censure nature and necessity. [. . .] To perceive all this can be very painful, but then comes a consolation: such pains are birth-pangs. The butterfly wants to get out of its cocoon, it tears at it, it breaks it open: then it is blinded and confused by the unfamiliar light, the realm of freedom. It is in such men as are *capable* of that suffering—how few they will be!—that the first attempt will be made to see whether mankind could *transform itself from a moral to a wise mankind.* [. . .] Everything is necessity—thus says the new knowledge; and this knowledge itself is necessity. Everything is innocence: and knowledge is the path to insight into this innocence. If pleasure, egoism, vanity are *necessary* for the production of the moral phenomena and their finest flower, the sense for truth and justice in knowledge; if error and aberration of the imagination was the only means by which mankind was able gradually to raise itself to this degree of self-enlightenment and self-redemption—who could venture to denigrate those means? Who could be despondent when he becomes aware of the goal to which those paths lead? It is true that everything in the domain of morality has become and is changeable, unsteady, everything is in flux: but *everything is also flooding forward*, and towards *one* goal. Even if the inherited habit of erroneous evaluation, loving, hating does continue to rule in us, under the influence of increasing knowledge it will grow weaker: a new habit, that of comprehending, not-loving, not-hating, surveying is gradually implanting itself in us on the same soil and will in thousands of years' time perhaps be strong enough to bestow on mankind the power of bringing forth the wise, innocent (conscious of innocence) man as regularly as it now brings forth—*not his antithesis but necessary preliminary*—the unwise, unjust, guilt-conscious man.

[HA 107]

132

We aeronauts of the spirit! —All those brave birds which fly out into the distance, into the farthest distance—it is certain! somewhere or other they will be unable to go on and will perch down on a mast or a bare cliff-face—and they will even be thankful for this miserable accommodation! But who could venture to infer from that, that there was *not* an immense open space before them, that they had flown as far as one *could* fly! All our great teachers and predecessors have at last come to a stop [. . .] it will be the same with you and me! But what does that matter

to you and me! *Other birds will fly farther!* This insight
and faith of ours [. . .] surveys the distance and sees
before it the flocks of birds which, far stronger than we,
still strive whither we have striven, and where everything
is sea, sea, sea! —And whither then would we go? Would
we *cross* the sea? Whither does this mighty longing draw
us, this longing that is worth more than any pleasure?
Why just in this direction, thither where all the suns of
humanity have hitherto *gone down*? Will it perhaps be
said of us one day that we too, *steering westward, hoped
to reach an India*—but that it was our fate to be wrecked
against infinity? Or, my brothers. Or?

[D 575]

133

Horizon: infinity.—We have left the land and taken to
our ship! We have burned our bridges—more, we have
burned our land behind us! Now, little ship, take care!
The ocean lies all around you; true, it is not always roar-
ing, and sometimes it lies there as if it were silken and
golden and a gentle favourable dream. But there will be
times when you will know that it is infinite and that there
is nothing more terrible than infinity [. . .]

[GS 124]

134

Excelsior! —'You will never again pray, never again worship, never again repose in limitless trust—you deny it to
yourself to remain halted before an ultimate wisdom,
ultimate good, ultimate power, and there unharness your
thoughts [. . .] [T]here is no longer for you any rewarder
and recompenser, no final corrector—there is no longer
any reason in what happens, no longer any love in what
happens to you—there is no longer any resting-place

open to your heart where it has only to find and no
longer to seek, you resist any kind of ultimate peace [. . .]
[W]ill you renounce in all this? Who will give you the
strength for it? No one has yet possessed this
strength!'—There is a lake which one day denied it to
itself to flow away and threw up a dam at the place
where it formerly flowed away: since then this lake has
risen higher and higher. Perhaps it is precisely that
renunciation which will also lend us the strength by
which the renunciation itself can be endured; perhaps
man will rise higher and higher from that time when he
no longer *flows out* into a God.

[GS 285]

135

[. . .] Let where you are going, not where you come form,
henceforth be your honour! [. . .]

O my brothers, your nobility shall not gaze backward, but *outward*! You shall be fugitives from all father-
lands and forefatherlands!

You shall love your *children's land*: let this love be
your new nobility—the undiscovered land in the furthest
sea! I bid your sails seek it and seek it!

You shall *make amends* to your children for being
the children of your fathers: *thus* you shall redeem all
that is past! This new law-table do I put over you!

[Z III *Of Old and New Law-Tables* 12]

136

The background of our cheerfulness. The greatest recent
event—that "God is dead," that the belief in the Christian
God has ceased to be believable—is even now beginning
to cast its first shadows over Europe. [. . .] In the main,
however, this [. . .] event itself is much too great, too

distant, too far from the comprehension of the many even for the tidings of it to be thought of as having *arrived* yet, not to speak of the notion that many people might know what has really happened here, and what must collapse now that this belief has been undermined—all that was built upon it, leaned on it, grew into it; for example, our whole European morality. . . .

[. . .] Why is it that even we look forward to it without any [. . .] worry and fear for *ourselves*? Is it perhaps that [. . .] the first consequences of this event [. . .] are perhaps the reverse of what one might expect: not at all sad and dark, but rather like a new, scarcely describable kind of light, happiness, relief, exhilaration, encouragement, dawn? Indeed, we philosophers and "free spirits" feel as if a new dawn were shining on us when we receive the tidings that "the old god is dead"; our heart overflows with gratitude, amazement, anticipation, expectation. At last the horizon appears free again to us, even granted that it is not bright; at last our ships may venture out again, venture out to face any danger; all the daring of the lover of knowledge is permitted again; the sea, *our* sea, lies open again; perhaps there has never yet been such an "open sea."

[GS 343 (1887)]

137

[. . .] But the struggle against Plato, or, to express it more plainly [. . .], the struggle against the Christian-ecclesiastical pressure of millennia—for Christianity is Platonism for 'the people'—has created in Europe a magnificent tension of the spirit such as has never existed on earth before: with so tense a bow one can now shoot for the most distant targets. [. . .]

[BGE *Preface*]

138

With the strength of his spiritual sight and insight the [. . .]
space [. . .] around man continually expands: his world
grows deeper, ever new stars, ever new images and enig-
mas come into view. Perhaps everything on which the
spirit's eye has exercised its profundity and acuteness has
been really but an opportunity for its exercise, a game,
something for children and the childish. Perhaps the
most solemn concepts which have occasioned the most
strife and suffering, the concepts 'God' and 'sin', will one
day seem to us of no more importance than a child's toy
and a child's troubles seem to an old man—and perhaps
'old man' will then have need of another toy and other
troubles—still enough of a child, an eternal child!

[BGE 57]

New Tasks

139

Distant prospect.—If only those actions are moral which
are performed for the sake of another [. . .], as one definition has it, then there are no moral actions! If only those
actions are moral which are performed out of freedom of
will, as another definition says, then there are likewise
no moral actions!—What is it then which is so *named*
and which in any event exists and wants explaining? It is
the effects of certain intellectual mistakes.—And supposing one freed oneself from these errors, what would
become of 'moral actions'? [. . .] Will they from then on
be performed less often because they are now valued
less highly?—Inevitably! [. . .] But our counter-reckoning
is that we shall restore to men their goodwill towards the
actions decried as egoistic and restore to these actions

their *value—we shall deprive them of their bad conscience!* And since they have hitherto been by far the
most frequent actions, and will continue to be so for all
future time, we thus remove from the entire aspect of
action and life its *evil appearance!* This is a very signifi-
cant result! When man no longer regards himself as evil
he ceases to be so!

[D 148]

140

On board ship!—If one considers the effect on every
individual of a philosophical total justification of his way
of living and thinking—it is like a warming, scorching,
fructifying sun which shines especially for him, it makes
him indifferent to praise or blame, self-contented, rich,
generous with happiness and benevolence, it constantly
transforms evil to good, brings all his forces to blossom
and ripeness and forbids the small and great weeds of
anger and vexation to flourish—then one at last cries out:
oh that many such new suns might be created! [. . .]
There is another new world to discover—and more than
one! On board ship, philosophers!

[GS 289]

141

The great health.—We new, nameless, ill-understood pre-
mature-born of a yet undemonstrated future—we need
for a new goal also a new means, namely a new health,
a stronger, shrewder, tougher, more daring, more cheerful health than any has been hitherto. [. . .]—it seems to
us as if we have [. . .] a yet undiscovered country before
us whose boundaries none has ever seen, a land beyond
all known lands and corners of the ideal, a world so
over-full of the beautiful, strange, questionable, terrible

and divine that our curiosity and our thirst for possession are both beside themselves—so that nothing can any longer satisfy us! How, after such prospects and with such a ravenous hunger in conscience and knowledge, could we remain content with the *man of the present*? [. . .]

[GS 382]

142

We, who have a different faith—we, to whom the democratic movement is not merely a form assumed by political organization in decay but also a form assumed by man in decay, [. . .] in process of becoming mediocre and losing his value: whither must *we* direct our hopes?—Towards *new philosophers*, we have no other choice; towards spirits strong and original enough [. . .] to revalue and reverse 'eternal values': towards [. . .] men of the future who in the present knot together the constraint which compels the will of millennia on to *new* paths. To teach man the future of man as his *will*, as dependent on a human will [. . .] It is the image of such leaders which hovers before *our* eyes—may I say that aloud, you free spirits? The circumstances one would have in part to create, in part to employ, to bring them into existence; the conjectural paths and tests by virtue of which a soul could grow to such height and power it would feel *compelled* to these tasks; a revaluation of values under whose novel pressure and hammer a conscience would be steeled, a heart transformed to brass, so that it might endure the weight of such a responsibility; on the other hand, the need for such leaders, the terrible danger they might not appear or might fail or might degenerate—these are *our* proper cares and concerns, do you know that, you free spirits? [. . .] The *collective degeneration of man* down to that which the socialist dolts and blockheads today see as their 'man of the future'—as their ideal!—this degeneration and diminution of man to the perfect herd animal (or, as they say, to the man of the 'free society'), this animalization of man to the pygmy animal of equal rights and equal pretensions is *possible*, there is no doubt about that! He who has once thought this possibility through to the end knows one more kind of disgust than other men do—and perhaps also a new *task!* . . .

[BGE 203]

143

I insist that philosophical labourers and men of science in general should once and for all cease to be confused with philosophers [. . .]. It may be required for the education of a philosopher that he himself has also once stood on all those steps on which his servants, the scientific labourers of philosophy, remain standing—*have* to remain standing; he himself must perhaps have been critic and sceptic and dogmatist and historian and, in addition, poet and [. . .] reader of riddles and moralist [. . .] and practically everything, so as to traverse the whole range of human values and value-feelings and be *able* to gaze from the heights into every distance [. . .]. But all these are only preconditions of his task: this task itself demands something different—it demands that he *create values*. Those philosophical labourers after the noble exemplar of Kant and Hegel have to take [. . .] former *assessments* of value, creations of value which have become dominant and are for a while called 'truths'—and identify them and reduce them to formulas [. . .]. It is the duty of these scholars to take everything that has hitherto happened and been valued, and make it

clear, distinct, intelligible and manageable, to abbreviate
everything [. . .] and to *subdue* the entire past: a tremendous and wonderful task in the service of which every
subtle pride, every tenacious will can certainly find satisfaction. *Actual philosophers, however, are commanders
and law-givers*: they say 'thus it *shall* be!', it is they who
determine the Wherefore and Whither of mankind, and
they possess for this task the preliminary work of all
those who have subdued the past—they reach for the
future with creative hand, and everything that is or has
been becomes for them a means, an instrument, a hammer. Their 'knowing' is *creating*, their creating is a law-
giving, their will to truth is—*will to power*.—Are there
such philosophers today? Have there been such philosophers? *Must* there not be such philosophers? . . .

[BGE 211]

144

It seems to me more and more that the philosopher,
being *necessarily* a man of tomorrow and the day after
tomorrow, has always found himself and *had* to find
himself in contradiction to his today [. . .]. Hitherto [. . .]
philosophers [. . .] have found their task, their hard,
unwanted, unavoidable task, but finally the greatness of
their task, in being the bad conscience of their age. By
laying the knife vivisectionally to the bosom of the very
virtues of the age they betrayed what was their own
secret: to know a *new* greatness of man, a new untrod-
den path to his enlargement. [. . .]

[BGE 212]

145

[. . .] it would be nicer if, instead of with cruelty, we were perhaps credited with an 'extravagant honesty'—we free, *very* free spirits—and perhaps *that* will actually one day be our posthumous fame? In the meantime—for it will be a long time before that happens—we ourselves are likely to be least inclined to dress up in moralistic verbal tinsel [. . .]. They are beautiful, glittering, jingling, festive words: honesty, love of truth, love of wisdom, sacrifice for the sake of knowledge, heroism of the truthful—there is something about them that makes one's pride swell. But we hermits and marmots long ago became convinced that this worthy verbal pomp too belongs among the ancient false finery, lumber and gold-dust of unconscious human vanity, and that under such flattering colours and varnish too the terrible basic text *homo natura* must again be discerned. For to translate man back into nature; to master the many vain and fanciful interpretations and secondary meanings which have been hitherto scribbled and daubed over that eternal basic text *homo natura*; to confront man henceforth with man in the way in which, hardened by the discipline of science, man today confronts the *rest* of nature, with dauntless Oedipus eyes and stopped-up Odysseus ears, deaf to the siren songs of old metaphysical bird-catchers who have all too long been piping to him 'you are more! you are higher! you are of a different origin!'—that may be a strange and extravagant task but it is a *task*—who would deny that? [. . .]

[BGE 230]

146

[. . .] Man has all too long had an "evil eye" for his natural inclinations, so that they have finally become inseparable from his "bad conscience." An attempt at the reverse

would *in itself* be possible—but who is strong enough
for it?—that is, to wed the bad conscience to all the
unnatural inclinations, all those aspirations to the
beyond, to that which runs counter to sense, instinct,
nature, animal, in short all ideals hitherto, which are one
and all hostile to life and ideals that slander the world.
To whom should one turn today with *such* hopes and
demands?

[GM 2.24]

147

[. . .] The peculiar, withdrawn attitude of the philosopher,
world-denying, hostile to life, suspicious of the senses,
[. . .] which has [. . .] become virtually the *philosopher's
pose par excellence*—it is above all a result of the emer-
gency conditions under which philosophy arose and sur-
vived at all; for the longest time philosophy would not
have been *possible at all* on earth without ascetic wraps
and cloak, without an ascetic self-misunderstanding. To
put it vividly: the *ascetic priest* provided until the most
modern times the repulsive and gloomy caterpillar form
in which alone the philosopher could live and creep
about.

  [. . .] Has that many-colored and dangerous winged
creature, the "spirit" which this caterpillar concealed,
really been unfettered at last and released into the light,
thanks to a sunnier, warmer, brighter world? Is there sufficient pride, daring, courage, self-confidence, available
today, sufficient will of the spirit, will to reponsibility,
freedom of will, for "the philosopher" to be henceforth
—*possible* on earth?—

[GM 3.10]

Higher Humanity

The Higher Human (Superman)

148

[. . .] We, however, *want to be those who* [. . .] give themselves their own law, those who create themselves! [. . .]

[GS 335]

149

[. . .] *I teach you the Superman.* Man is something that should be overcome. What have you done to overcome him?

All creatures hitherto have created something beyond themselves: and do you want to be the ebb of this great tide, and return to the animals rather than overcome man?

What is the ape to men? A laughing-stock or a painful embarrassment. And just so shall man be to the Superman [. . .]

You have made your way from worm to man, and much in you is still worm. Once you were apes, and even now man is more of an ape than any ape. [. . .]

The Superman is the meaning of the earth. Let your will say: The Superman *shall be* the meaning of the earth! [. . .]

[Z I *Prologue* 3]

150

[. . .] Man is a rope, fastened between animal and Superman—a rope over an abyss. [. . .]

[Z I *Prologue* 4]

151

[. . .] And this is the great noontide: it is when man stands at the middle of his course between animal and Superman [. . .]

'*All gods are dead: now we want the Superman to live*'—let this be our last will one day at the great noontide!

[Z I *Of the Bestowing Virtue* 3]

152

[. . .] Once you said 'God' when you gazed upon distant seas; but now I have taught you to say 'Superman'.

[Z II *On the Blissful Islands*]

153

[. . .] You Higher Men, learn this from me: In the market-place no one believes in Higher Men. And if you want to speak there, very well, do so! But the mob blink and say: 'We are all equal.'

'You Higher Men'—thus the mob blink—'there are no Higher Men, we are all equal, man is but man, before God—we are all equal!'

Before God! But now this God has died. And let us

not be equal before the mob. You Higher Men, depart from the marketplace!

[. . .] You Higher Men, this God was your greatest danger.

Only since he has lain in the grave have you again been resurrected. [. . .]

[. . .] now *we* desire—that the Superman shall live.

[Z IV *Of the Higher Man* 1,2]

154

The most cautious people ask today: 'How may man still be preserved?' Zarathustra, however, asks as the sole and first one to do so: 'How shall man be *overcome?*'

The Superman lies close to my heart, *he* is my paramount and sole concern—and *not* man: not the nearest, not the poorest, not the most suffering, not the best. [. . .]

That you have despised, you Higher Men, that makes me hope. For the great despisers are the great reverers.

That you have despaired, there is much honour in that. For you have not learned how to submit, you have not learned petty prudence.

For today the petty people have become lord and master: they all preach submission and acquiescence and prudence and diligence and consideration and the long *et cetera* of petty virtues. [. . .]

'How may man preserve himself best, longest, most agreeably?' With that—they are the masters of the present.

Overcome for me these masters of the present, O my brothers—these petty people: *they* are the Superman's greatest danger!

Overcome, you Higher Men, the petty virtues, the petty prudences, the sand-grain discretion, the ant-swarm

inanity, miserable ease, the 'happiness of the greatest
number'!

And rather despair than submit. [. . .]

[Z IV *Of the Higher Man* 3]

155

One may conjecture that a spirit in whom the type 'free
spirit' will one day become ripe and sweet to the point of
perfection has had its decisive experience in a *great liberation* and that previously it was [. . .] a fettered spirit
[. . .]. What fetters the fastest? What bonds are all but
unbreakable? In the case of men of a high and select
kind they will be their duties: that reverence proper to
youth, that reserve and delicacy before all that is hon-
oured and revered from of old, that gratitude for the soil
out of which they have grown, for the hand which led
them, for the holy place where they learned to worship—their supreme moments themselves will fetter
them the fastest, lay upon them the most enduring obligation. The great liberation comes for those who are thus
fettered suddenly, like the shock of an earthquake: the
youthful soul is all at once convulsed, torn loose, torn
away—[. . .] 'Better to die than to go on living
here'—thus resounds the imperious voice and temptation: and this 'here', this 'at home' is everything it had
hitherto loved! A sudden terror and suspicion of what it
loved, a lightning-bolt of contempt for what it called
'duty', a rebellious arbitrary, volcanically erupting desire
for travel, strange places, estrangement, coldness, sober-
ness, frost, a hatred for love, perhaps a desecrating blow
and glance *backwards* to where it formerly loved and
worshipped, perhaps a hot blush of shame at what it has
just done and at the same time an exultation *that* it has

done it, a drunken, inwardly exultant shudder which betrays that a victory has been won—a victory? over what? over whom? an enigmatic, question-packed, questionable victory, but the *first* victory nonetheless: such bad and painful things are part of the history of the great liberation. [. . .]

From this morbid isolation, from the desert of these years of temptation and experiment, it is still a long road to that[. . .] *mature* freedom of spirit which is equally self-mastery and discipline of the heart and permits access to many and contradictory modes of thought— [. . . to] that superfluity which grants to the free spirit the dangerous privilege of living *experimentally* and of being allowed to offer itself to adventure: the master's privilege of the free spirit! [. . .]

[. . .] If he has for long hardly dared to ask himself: 'why so apart so alone? renouncing everything I once reverenced? renouncing reverence itself? Why this hardness, this suspiciousness[. . .]?'—now he dares to ask it aloud and hears in reply something like an answer. 'You shall become master over yourself, master also over your virtues. Formerly *they* were your masters; but they must be only your instruments beside other instruments. [. . .] from now on the free spirit *knows* what 'you shall' he has obeyed, and he also knows what he now *can*, what only now he—*may* do . . .

[HA *Preface* 3–6 (1886)]

156

Jesus said to his Jews: 'The law was made for servants— love God as I love him, as his son! What have we sons of God to do with morality!'—

[BGE 164]

157

[. . .] Another ideal runs ahead of us, a strange, seductive, dangerous ideal to which we do not want to convert anyone because we do not easily admit that anyone has a *right to it*: the ideal of a spirit who [. . .] from overflowing plenitude and power, plays with everything hitherto called holy, good, untouchable, divine; for whom the highest things by which the people reasonably enough take their standards would signify something like a danger, a corruption, a degradation, or at least a recreation, a blindness, a temporary self-forgetfulness; the ideal of a human-superhuman well-being and well-wishing which will often enough seem *inhuman*, for example when it is set beside the whole of earthly seriousness hitherto [. . .]

[GS 382 (1887)]

158

[. . .] To be incapable of taking one's enemies, one's accidents, even one's misdeeds seriously for very long—that is the sign of strong, full natures in whom there is an excess of the power to form, to mold, to recuperate and to forget [. . .] Such a man shakes off with a *single* shrug many vermin that eat deep into others; here alone genuine "love of one's enemies" is possible—supposing it to be possible at all on earth. How much reverence has a noble man for his enemies!—and such reverence is a bridge to love. [. . .]

[GM 1.10]

159

[. . .] But some day, in a stronger age than this decaying, self-doubting present, he must yet come to us, the *redeeming* man of great love and contempt, the creative spirit whose compelling strength will not let him rest in any aloofness or any beyond, whose isolation is misunderstood by the people as if it were flight *from* reality—while it is only his absorption, immersion, penetration *into* reality, so that, when he one day emerges again into the light, he may bring home the *redemption* of this reality: its redemption from the curse that the hitherto reigning ideal has laid upon it. This man of the future, who will redeem us not only from the hitherto reigning ideal but also from that which was bound to grow out of it, the great nausea, the will to nothingness, nihilism; this bell-stroke of noon and of the great decision that liberates the will again and restores its goal to the earth and his hope to man; this Antichrist and antinihilist; this victor over God and nothingness—*he must come one day.—*

[GM 2.24]

The School of Self-Overcoming

160

A kind of cult of the passions.—[. . .] It [. . .] is up to us [. . .] to *take from* the passions their terrible character and thus prevent their becoming devastating torrents.—[. . .] let us [. . .] work honestly together on the task of transforming the passions [*Leidenschaften*] of mankind one and all into joys [*Freudenschaften*].

[WS 37]

161

Overcoming of the passions.—The man who has overcome his passions has entered into possession of the most fertile ground; like the colonist who has mastered the forests and swamps. To *sow* the seeds of good spiritual works in the soil of the subdued passions is then the immediate urgent task. The overcoming itself is only a *means*, not a goal; if it is not so viewed, all kinds of weeds and devilish nonsense will quickly spring up in this rich soil now unoccupied, and soon there will be more rank confusion than there ever was before.

[WS 53]

162

Preserver of the species.—It is the strongest and most evil spirits who have up till now advanced mankind the most [. . .]—they have awoken again and again the sense of [. . .] joy in the new, daring, untried, they have compelled men to set opinion against opinion, model against model. Most of all by weapons, by overturning boundary stones, by wounding piety: but also by new religions and moralities! The same 'wickedness' is in every teacher and preacher of the new as makes a conqueror infamous [. . .] The new, however, is under all circumstances the evil, as that which wants to conquer and overturn the old boundary stones and the old pieties; and only the old is the good! The good men of every age are those who bury the old ideas in the depths of the earth and bear fruit with them, the agriculturalists of the spirit. But that land will at length become exhausted, and the ploughshare of evil must come again and again. [. . .] In truth [. . .], the evil impulses are just as useful, indispensable and preservative of the species as the good:—only their function is different.

[GS 4]

163

Evil.—Examine the lives of the best and most fruitful men and peoples, and ask yourselves whether a tree, if it is to grow proudly into the sky, can do without bad weather and storms: whether unkindness and opposition from without, whether some sort of hatred, envy, obstinacy, mistrust, severity, greed and violence do not belong to the *favouring* circumstances without which a great increase even in virtue is hardly possible. The poison which destroys the weaker nature strengthens the stronger—and he does not call it poison, either.

[GS 19]

164

Preparatory men.—I greet all the signs that a more manly, warlike age is coming, which will [. . .] *wage war* for the sake of ideas and their consequences. To that end many brave pioneers are needed now [. . .] men who know how to be silent, solitary, resolute, [. . .] who have an innate disposition to seek in all things that which must be *overcome* in them: men to whom cheerfulness, patience, simplicity and contempt for the great vanities belong just as much as do generosity in victory and indulgence towards the little vanities of the defeated: [. . .] men with their own festivals, their own work-days, their own days of mourning, accustomed to and assured in command and equally ready to obey when necessary, equally proud in the one case as in the other, equally serving their own cause: men more imperilled, men more fruitful, happier men! For believe me!—the secret of realizing the greatest fruitfulness and the greatest enjoyment of existence is: to *live dangerously*! Build your cities on the slopes of Vesuvius! Send your ships out into uncharted seas! Live in conflict with your equals and with your-.

selves! Be robbers and ravagers as long as you cannot be rulers and owners, you men of knowledge! [. . .]

[GS 283]

165

To those who preach morals.—I do not wish to promote any morality, but to those who do I give this advice: If you wish to deprive the best things and states of all honor and worth, then go on talking about them as you have been doing. Place them at the head of your morality and talk from morning to night of the happiness of virtue, the composure of the soul, of justice and immanent retribution. The way you are going about it, all these good things will eventually have popularity and the clamor of the streets on their side; but at the same time all the gold that was on them will have been worn off by so much handling, and all the gold *inside* will have turned to lead. Truly, you are masters of alchemy in reverse: the devaluation of what is most valuable. Why don't you make the experiment of trying another prescription to keep from attaining the opposite of your goal as you have done hitherto? *Deny* these good things, withdraw the mob's acclaim from them as well as their easy currency; make them once again concealed secrets of solitary souls; say *that morality is something forbidden.* That way you might win over for these things the kind of people who alone matter: I mean those who are *heroic.* [. . .] Hasn't the time come to say of morality what Master Eckhart said: "I ask God to rid me of God."

[GS 292]

166

[. . .] Let us divinely strive *against* one another!

[Z II *Of the Tarantulas*]

167

Every morality is, as opposed to *laisser aller*, a piece of
tyranny against 'nature', likewise against 'reason': but that
can be no objection to it unless one is in possession of
some other morality which decrees that any kind of
tyranny and unreason is impermissible. The essential and
invaluable element in every morality is that it is a protracted constraint [. . .] [T]he strange fact is that all there is
or has been on earth of freedom, subtlety, boldness, [. . .]
whether in thinking itself, or in ruling, or in speaking and
persuasion, [. . .] has evolved only by virtue of the 'tyranny of such arbitrary laws'; and, in all seriousness, there is
no small probability that precisely this is 'nature' and
'natural'—and *not* that *laisser aller*! [. . .] The essential
thing 'in heaven and upon earth' seems, to say it again,
to be a protracted *obedience* in *one* direction: from out of
that there always emerges and has always emerged in the
long run something for the sake of which it is worth-
while to live on earth, for example virtue, art, music,
dance, reason, spirituality—something transfiguring,
refined, mad and divine.

[BGE 188]

168

Whether it be hedonism or pessimism or utilitarianism or
eudaemonism: all these modes of thought which assess
the value of things according to *pleasure* and *pain*, that
is to say according to attendant and secondary phenomena, are foreground modes of thought and naïveties which
anyone conscious of *creative* powers and an artist's conscience will look down on with derision [. . .] You want if
possible—and there is no madder 'if possible'—*to abolish suffering*; and we?—it really does seem that *we* would
rather increase it and make it worse than it has ever

been! Wellbeing as you understand it—that is no goal, that seems to us an *end*! A state which soon renders man ludicrous and contemptible—which makes it *desirable* that he should perish! The discipline of suffering, of *great* suffering—do you not know that it is *this* discipline alone which has created every elevation of mankind hitherto? That tension of the soul in misfortune which cultivates its strength, its terror at the sight of great destruction, its inventiveness and bravery in undergoing, enduring, interpreting, exploiting misfortune, and whatever of depth, mystery, mask, spirit, cunning and greatness has been bestowed upon it—has it not been bestowed through suffering? [. . .]

[BGE 225]

169

[. . .] Every animal—therefore *la bête philosophe*, too—instinctively strives for an optimum of favorable conditions under which it can expend all its strength and achieve its maximal feeling of power; every animal abhors, just as instinctively and with a subtlety of discernment that is "higher than all reason," every kind of intrusion or hindrance that obstructs or could obstruct this path to the optimum [. . .] Thus the philosopher abhors *marriage* [. . .]. What great philosopher hitherto has been married? Heraclitus, Plato, Descartes, Spinoza, Leibniz, Kant, Schopenhauer—they were not; more, one cannot even *imagine* them married. A married philosopher belongs *in comedy*, that is my proposition—and as for that exception, Socrates—the malicious Socrates, it would seem, married *ironically*, just to demonstrate *this* proposition.

[. . .] Ascetic ideals reveal so many bridges to *independence* that a philosopher is bound to rejoice and clap his hands when he hears that story of all those resolute men who one day said No to all servitude and went into some *desert*: even supposing they were merely strong asses and quite the reverse of a strong spirit.

What, then, is the meaning of the ascetic ideal in the case of a philosopher? My answer is—you will have guessed it long ago: the philosopher sees in it an optimum condition for the highest and boldest spirituality and smiles—he does *not* deny "existence," he rather affirms *his* existence and *only* his existence, and this perhaps to the point at which he is not far from harboring the impious wish: *pereat mundus, fiat philosophia, fiat philosophus*, **fiam!**[1]

As you see, they are not unbiased witnesses and judges of the *value* of the ascetic ideal, these philosophers! They think of *themselves*—what is "the saint" to them! They think of what *they* can least do without: freedom from compulsion, disturbance, noise, from tasks, duties, worries; clear heads; the dance, leap, and flight of ideas; good air, thin, clear, open, dry, like the air of the heights through which all animal being becomes more spiritual and acquires wings; repose in all cellar regions; all dogs nicely chained up; no barking of hostility and shaggy-haired rancor; no gnawing worm of injured ambition; undemanding and obedient intestines, busy as windmills but distant; the heart remote, beyond, heavy with future, posthumous—all in all, they think of the ascetic ideal as the cheerful asceticism of an animal become fledged and divine, floating above life rather than in repose. [. . .]

We have seen how a certain asceticism, a severe and cheerful continence with the best will, belongs to the most favorable conditions of supreme spirituality, and is also among its most natural consequences [. . .]

[. . .] [L]ife wrestles in [. . .] and through [the ascetic ideal] with death and *against* death; the ascetic ideal is an artifice for the *preservation* of life. [. . .]

[GM 3.7, 8, 9, 13]

170

From the military school of life.—What does not kill me makes me stronger.

[T *Maxims and Arrows* 8]

171

[. . .] Learning to *see*—habituating the eye to repose, to patience, to letting things come to it; learning to defer judgement, to investigate and comprehend the individual case in all its aspects. This is the *first* preliminary schooling in spirituality: *not* to react immediately to a stimulus, but to have the restraining, stock-taking instincts in one's control. Learning to *see*, as I understand it, is almost what is called in unphilosophical language 'strong will-power': the essence of it is precisely *not* to 'will', the *ability* to defer decision. All unspirituality, all vulgarity, is due to the incapacity to resist a stimulus—one *has* to react, one obeys every impulse. In many instances, such a compulsion is already morbidity, decline, a symptom of exhaustion—almost everything which unphilosophical crudity designates by the name 'vice' is merely this physiological incapacity *not* to react.—[. . .]

[T *What the Germans Lack* 6]

172

[. . .] For what is freedom? That one has the will to self-responsibility. That one preserves the distance which divides us. That one has become more indifferent to hardship, toil, privation, even to life. That one is ready to sacrifice men to one's cause, oneself not excepted. Freedom means that the manly instincts that delight in war and victory have gained mastery over the other instincts—for example, over the instinct for 'happiness'. The man *who has become free*—and how much more the *mind* that has become free—spurns the contemptible sort of well-being dreamed of by shopkeepers, Christians, cows, women, Englishmen, and other democrats. The free man is a *warrior*.—How is freedom measured, in individuals as in nations? By the resistance which has to be overcome, by the effort it costs to stay *aloft*. One would have to seek the highest type of free man where the greatest resistance is constantly being overcome [. . .] *First* principle: one must need strength, otherwise one will never have it. [. . .]

[T *Expeditions of an Untimely Man* 38]

The Creative Will

173

'*Will a self*'.—Active, successful natures act, not according to the dictum 'know thyself', but as if there hovered before them the commandment: *will* a self and thou shalt *become* a self. [. . .]

[AOM 366]

174

[. . .] Truly, men have given themselves all their good and evil. Truly, they did not take it, they did not find it, it did not descend to them as a voice from heaven.

Man first implanted values into things to maintain himself—he created the meaning of things, a human meaning! Therefore he calls himself: 'Man', that is: the evaluator.

Evaluation is creation: hear it, you creative men! Valuating is itself the value and jewel of all valued things.

Only through evaluation is there value: and without evaluation the nut of existence would be hollow. Hear it, you creative men! [. . .]

[Z I *Of the Thousand and One Goals*]

175

The figs are falling from the trees, they are fine and sweet; and as they fall their red skins split. I am a north wind to ripe figs.

Thus, like figs, do these teachings fall to you, my friends: now drink their juice and eat their sweet flesh! It is autumn all around and clear sky and afternoon.

Behold, what abundance is around us! And it is fine to gaze out upon distant seas from the midst of superfluity.

Once you said 'God' when you gazed upon distant seas; but now I have taught you to say 'Superman'.

God is a supposition; but I want your supposing to reach no further than your creating will.

Could you *create* a god?—So be silent about all gods! But you could surely create the Superman.

Perhaps not yourselves, my brothers! But you could transform yourselves into forefathers and ancestors of the Superman: and let this be your finest creating! [. . .]

Willing liberates: that is the true doctrine of will and freedom—thus Zarathustra teaches you. [. . .]

This will lured me away from God and gods; for what would there be to create if gods—existed! [. . .]

[Z II *On the Blissful Islands*]

176

[. . .] Will—that is what the liberator and bringer of joy is called: thus I have taught you, my friends! But now learn this as well: The will itself is still a prisoner.

Willing liberates: but what is it that fastens in fetters even the liberator?

'It was': that is what the will's teeth-gnashing and most lonely affliction is called. Powerless against that which has been done, the will is an angry spectator of all things past.

The will cannot will backwards; that it cannot break time and time's desire—that is the will's most lonely affliction. [. . .]

Until the creative will says to [the past]: 'But I will it thus! Thus shall I will it!'

But has it ever spoken thus? [. . .]

[. . .] Who has taught it to will backwards, too?[2]

[Z II *Of Redemption*]

177

[. . .] Oh, that you would put from you all *half* willing [. . .]

Oh, that you understood my saying: 'Always do what you will—but first be such as *can will*!' [. . .]

[Z III *Of the Virtue that Makes Small 3*]

178

[. . .] And that is always the nature of weak men: they lose themselves on their way. And at last their weariness asks: 'Why have we ever taken any way? It is a matter of indifference!'

It sounds pleasant to *their* ears when it is preached: 'Nothing is worth while! You shall not will!' This, however, is a sermon urging slavery. [. . .]

Willing liberates: for willing is creating: thus I teach. And you should learn *only* for creating!

[Z III *Of Old and New Law-Tables* 16]

179

[. . .] Nothing more gladdening grows on earth, O Zarathustra, than an exalted, robust will: it is the earth's fairest growth. A whole landscape is refreshed by one such tree. [. . .]

[Z IV *The Greeting*]

180

[. . .] If we place ourselves at the end of this tremendous process [of the evolution of the inner life in the human animal], where the tree at last brings forth fruit, [. . .] then we discover that the ripest fruit is the *sovereign individual*, like only to himself, liberated again from morality of custom, autonomous and supramoral [. . .] in short, the man who has his own independent, protracted will and the *right to make promises*—and in him a proud consciousness, quivering in every muscle, of *what* has at length been achieved and become flesh in him, a consciousness of his own power and freedom, a sensation of mankind come to completion. This emancipated individual, with the actual *right* to make promises, this master of a *free* will, this sovereign man—how should he not be aware of his superiority over all those who lack the right to make promises and stand as their own guarantors [. . .]—and how this mastery over himself also necessarily gives him mastery over circumstances, over nature, and over all more short-willed and unreliable creatures? The "free" man, the possessor of a protracted and unbreakable will, also possesses his *measure of value* [. . .] The proud awareness of the extraordinary privilege of *responsibility*, the consciousness of this rare freedom, this power over oneself and over fate, has in his case penetrated to the profoundest depths and become instinct, the dominating instinct. What will he call this dominating instinct, supposing he feels the need to give it a name? The answer is beyond doubt: this sovereign man calls it his *conscience*.

[GM 2.2]

Healthy Selfishness

181

[. . .] For one thing is needful: that a human being attain his satisfaction with himself [. . .]; only then is a human being at all tolerable to behold. Whoever is dissatisfied with himself is always ready to revenge himself therefore; we others will be his victims, if only by always having to stand his ugly sight. For the sight of the ugly makes men bad and gloomy.

[GS 290 *Portable* 99]

182

[. . .] And then it also happened—and truly, it happened for the first time!—that his teaching glorified *selfishness*, the sound, healthy selfishness that issues from a mighty soul—

from a mighty soul, to which pertains the exalted body, the beautiful, victorious, refreshing body, around which everything becomes a mirror;

the supple, persuasive body, the dancer whose image and epitome is the self-rejoicing soul. [. . .]

Entirely hateful and loathsome to [my teaching] is he who will never defend himself, who swallows down poisonous spittle and evil looks, the too-patient man who puts up with everything, is content with everything: for that is the nature of slaves.

Whether one be servile before gods and divine kicks, or before men and the silly opinions of men: it spits at slaves of *all* kinds, this glorious selfishness! [. . .]

And he who declares the Ego healthy and holy and selfishness glorious—truly, he, a prophet, declares too what he knows: *'Behold, it comes, it is near, the great noontide!'*

[Z III *Of the Three Evil Things* 2]

183

You creators, you Higher Men! One is pregnant only with one's own child.

Let nothing impose upon you, nothing persuade you! For who is *your* neighbour? And if you do things 'for your neighbour', still you do not create for him!

Unlearn this 'for', you creators: your very virtue wants you to have nothing to do with 'for' and 'for the sake of' and 'because'. You should stop your ears to these false little words.

This 'for one's neighbour' is the virtue only of petty people: [. . .] they have neither right to nor strength for *your* selfishness!

The prudence and providence of pregnancy is in your selfishness! What no one has yet seen, the fruit: that is protected and indulged and nourished by your whole love. [. . .]

[Z IV *Of the Higher Man* 11]

---

¹ Let the world perish, but let there be philosophy, the philosopher, me!

² Nietzsche's proposed solution to the problem of how to "will backwards," that is, of how to affirm the totality of the past, is found in the doctrines of eternal recurrence and love of fate. See the first two sections of chapter 8.

Joyful Wisdom

[My teaching] despises all woeful wisdom [. . .]
which is always sighing: 'All is vain!'
[Z III *Of the Three Evil Things* 2]

Eternal Recurrence

184

The heaviest burden.—What if a demon crept after you
one day or night in your loneliest solitude and said to
you: 'This life, as you live it now and have lived it, you
will have to live again and again, times without number;
and there will be nothing new in it, but every pain and
every joy and every thought and sigh and all the
unspeakably small and great in your life must return to
you, and everything in the same series and
sequence—and in the same way this spider and this
moonlight among the trees, and in the same way this
moment and I myself. The eternal hour-glass of existence
will be turned again and again—and you with it, you
dust of dust!'—Would you not throw yourself down and
gnash your teeth and curse the demon who thus spoke?
Or have you experienced a tremendous moment in

which you would have answered him: 'You are a god and never did I hear anything more divine!' If this thought gained power over you it would, as you are now, transform and perhaps crush you; the question in all and everything: 'do you want this again and again, times without number?' would lie as the heaviest burden upon all your actions. Or how well disposed towards yourself and towards life would you have to become to have *no greater desire* than for this ultimate eternal sanction and seal?

[GS 341]

185

[. . .] 'Behold this gateway, dwarf!' I went on: 'it has two aspects. Two paths come together here: no one has ever reached their end.

'This long lane behind us: it goes on for an eternity. And that long lane ahead of us—that is another eternity.

[. . .] The name of the gateway is written above it: "Moment".

[. . .] 'Behold this moment!' I went on. 'From this gateway Moment a long, eternal lane runs *back*: an eternity lies behind us.

'Must not all things that *can* run have already run along this lane? Must not all things that *can* happen *have* already happened, been done, run past?

'And if all things have been here before: what do you think of this moment, dwarf? Must not this gateway, too, have been here—before?

'And are not all things bound fast together in such a way that this moment draws after it all future things? [. . .]

'For all things that *can* run *must* also run once again forward along this long lane.

'And this slow spider that creeps along in the moon-light, and this moonlight itself, and I and you at this gate-way whispering together, whispering of eternal things —must we not all have been here before?

'—and must we not return and run down that other lane out before us, down that long, terrible lane—must we not return eternally?' [. . .]

[Z III *Of the Vision and the Riddle* 2]

186

[. . .] 'Behold, we know what you teach: that all things recur eternally and we ourselves with them, and that we have already existed an infinite number of times before and all things with us.

'You teach that there is a great year of becoming, a colossus of a year: this year, must, like an hour-glass, turn itself over again and again, so that it may run down and run out anew [. . .]

'And if you should die now, O Zarathustra: behold, we know too what you would then say to yourself—[. . .]

'"Now I die and decay," you would say, "and in an instant I shall be nothingness. Souls are as mortal as bodies.

'"But the complex of causes in which I am entangled will recur—it will create me again! I myself am part of these causes of the eternal recurrence. [. . .]

'"I shall return eternally to this identical and self-same life, in the greatest things and in the smallest, to teach once more the eternal recurrence of all things,

'"to speak once more the teaching of the great noon-tide of earth and man, to tell man of the Superman once more. [. . .]'

[Z III *The Convalescent* 2]

187

[. . .] The doctrine of 'eternal recurrence', that is to say of the unconditional and endlessly repeated circular course of all things [. . .]

[EH *The Birth of Tragedy* 3]

188

[. . .] the *idea of eternal recurrence*, the highest formula of affirmation that can possibly be attained [. . .]

[EH *Thus Spoke Zarathustra* 1]

Redemption: The Sacred Yes and the Love of Fate

189

Consciousness of appearance.—In what a marvellous and new and at the same time terrible and ironic relationship with the totality of existence do I feel myself to stand with my knowledge! I have *discovered* for myself that the old human and animal world, indeed the entire prehistory and past of all sentient being, works on, loves on, hates on, thinks on in me—I have suddenly awoken in the midst of this dream but only to the consciousness that I am dreaming and that I *have* to go on dreaming in order not to be destroyed: as the sleepwalker has to go on dreaming in order not to fall. What is 'appearance' to me now! Certainly not the opposite of some kind of being—what can I possibly say about being of any kind that is not a predicate of its appearance! Certainly not a dead mask placed over an unknown 'x', which could, if one wished, be removed! Appearance is for me the active and living itself, which goes so far in its self-mockery as to allow me to feel that there is nothing here but appearance and will-o'-the-wisp and a flickering dance of spirits—that among all these dreamers I, too, the 'man of knowledge', dance my dance, that the man of knowledge is a means of spinning out the earthly dance and to that extent one of the masters-of-ceremonies of existence, and that the sublime consistency and unity of all knowledge is and will be perhaps the supreme means of *preserving* the universality of dreaming and the mutual intelligibility of all these dreamers, and thereby *the continuance of the dream*.

[GS 54]

190

For the New Year [1882]. I am still living, I am still thinking: I have to go on living because I have to go on thinking. *Sum, ergo cogito: cogito, ergo sum*. Today everyone is permitted to express his desire and dearest thoughts: so I too would like to say what I have desired of myself today and what thought was the first to cross my heart this year—what thought shall be the basis, guarantee and sweetness of all my future life! I want to learn more and more to see what is necessary in things as the beautiful in them—thus I shall become one of those who make things beautiful. *Amor fati*: may that be my love from now on! I want to wage no war against the ugly. I do not want to accuse, I do not want even to accuse the accusers. May *looking away* be my only form of negation! And, all in all: I want to be at all times hereafter only an affirmer [*ein Ja-sagender*]!

[GS 276]

191

I name you three metamorphoses of the spirit: how the
spirit shall become a camel, and the camel a lion, and
the lion at last a child. [. . .]

What is heavy? thus asks the weight-bearing spirit,
thus it kneels down like the camel and wants to be well
laden. [. . .]

The weight-bearing spirit takes upon itself all these
heaviest things: like a camel hurrying laden into the
desert [. . .]

But in the loneliest desert the second metamorpho-
sis occurs: the spirit here becomes a lion; it wants to cap-
ture freedom and be lord in its own desert. [. . .]

[I]t will struggle for victory with the great dragon.

What is the great dragon which the spirit no longer
wants to call lord and God? The great dragon is called
'Thou shalt'. But the spirit of the lion says 'I will!'

'Thou shalt' lies in its path, sparkling with gold, a
scale-covered beast, and on every scale glitters golden
'Thou shalt'.

Values of a thousand years glitter on the scales [. . .]

'All values have already been created, and all created values—are in me. Truly, there shall be no more "I
will"!' Thus speaks the dragon.

My brothers, why is the lion needed in the spirit?
Why does the beast of burden, that renounces and is rev-
erent, not suffice?

To create new values—even the lion is incapable of
that: but to create itself freedom for new creation—that
the might of the lion can do.

To create freedom for itself and a sacred No even to
duty: the lion is needed for that, my brothers. [. . .]

But tell me, my brothers, what can the child do that even the lion cannot? Why must the preying lion still become a child?

The child is innocence and forgetfulness, a new beginning, a sport, a self-propelling wheel, a first motion, a sacred Yes.

Yes, a sacred Yes is needed, my brothers, for the sport of creation: the spirit now wills *its own* will, the spirit sundered from the world now wins *its own* world. [. . .]

[Z I *Of the Three Metamorphoses*]

192

[. . .] I should believe only in a God who understood how to dance.

And when I beheld my devil, I found him serious, thorough, profound, solemn: it was the Spirit of Gravity—through him all things are ruined.

One does not kill by anger but by laughter. Come, let us kill the Spirit of Gravity! [. . .]

[Z I *Of Reading and Writing*]

193

[. . .] For *that man may be freed from the bonds of revenge*: that is the bridge to my highest hope and a rainbow after protracted storms.

[Z II *Of the Tarantulas*]

194

[. . .] To redeem the past and to transform every 'It was' into an 'I wanted it thus!'—that alone do I call redemption! [. . .]

[Z II *Of Redemption*]

195

[. . .] Striding mute over the mocking clatter of pebbles, trampling the stones that made it slip: thus my foot with effort forced itself upward.

Upward—despite the spirit that drew it downward, drew it towards the abyss, the Spirit of Gravity, my devil and arch-enemy.

Upward—although he sat upon me, half dwarf, half mole; crippled, crippling; pouring lead-drops into my ear, leaden thoughts into my brain.

'O Zarathustra,' he said mockingly, syllable by syllable, 'you stone of wisdom! You have thrown yourself high, but every stone that is thrown must—fall! [. . .]

But there is something in me that I call courage: it has always destroyed every discouragement in me. This courage at last bade me stop and say: 'Dwarf! You! Or I!' [. . .]

Courage [. . .] destroys even death, for it says: 'Was *that* life? Well then! Once more!'

But there is a great triumphant shout in such a saying. He who has ears to hear, let him hear.

[Z III *Of the Vision and the Riddle* 1]

196

[. . .] I [. . .] am one who blesses and declares Yes, if only you are around me, you pure, luminous sky! You abyss of light!—then into all abysses do I carry my consecrating declaration Yes. [. . .]

For all things are baptized at the fount of eternity and beyond good and evil; good and evil themselves, however, are only intervening shadows and damp afflictions and passing clouds.

Truly, it is a blessing and not a blasphemy when I teach: 'Above all things stands the heaven of chance, the heaven of innocence, the heaven of accident, the heaven of wantonness.'

'Lord Chance'—he is the world's oldest nobility, which I have given back to all things; I have released them from servitude under purpose.

I set this freedom and celestial cheerfulness over all things like an azure bell when I taught that no 'eternal will' acts over them and through them. [. . .]

O sky above me, you pure, lofty sky! This is now your purity to me, that there is no eternal reason-spider and spider's web in you—

that you are to me a dance floor for divine chances, that you are to me a gods' table for divine dice and dicers!

[Z III *Before Sunrise*]

197

[. . .] Did you ever say Yes to one joy? O my friends, then you said Yes to *all* woe as well. All things are chained and entwined together, all things are in love;

if ever you wanted one moment twice, if ever you said: 'You please me, happiness, instant, moment!' then you wanted *everything* to return!

you wanted everything anew, everything eternal, everything chained, entwined together, everything in love, O that is how you *loved* the world,

you everlasting men, loved it eternally, and for all time: and you say even to woe: 'Go, but return!' *For all joy wants—eternity!*

[Z IV *The Intoxicated Song* 10]

198

O Man! Attend!
What does deep midnight's voice contend?
'I slept my sleep,
'And now awake at dreaming's end:
'The world is deep,
'Deeper than day can comprehend.
'Deep is its woe,
'Joy—deeper than heart's agony:
'Woe says: Fade! Go!
'But all joy wants eternity,
'Wants deep, deep, deep eternity!'

[Z IV *The Intoxicated Song* 12]

199

[. . .] he who has really gazed with an Asiatic and more than Asiatic eye down into the most world-denying of all possible modes of thought—beyond good and evil and no longer, like Buddha and Schopenhauer, under the spell and illusion of morality—perhaps by that very act, and without really intending to, may have had his eyes opened to the opposite ideal: to the ideal of the most exuberant, most living and most world-affirming man, who has not only learned to get on and treat with all that was and is but who wants to have it again *as it was and is* to all eternity. . .

[BGE 56]

200

In every age the wisest have passed the identical judgement on life: *it is worthless.* . . . Everywhere and always their mouths have uttered the same sound—a sound full of doubt, full of melancholy, full of weariness with life, full of opposition to life. [. . .] Even Socrates had had enough of it.—What does that *prove*? What does it *point to*?—Formerly one would have said (—oh, and did say, and loudly enough, and our pessimists most of all!): 'Here at any rate there must be something true! The *consensus sapientium* is proof of truth.'—Shall we still speak thus today? are we *allowed* to do so? 'Here at any rate there must be something *sick*'—this is *our* retort: one ought to take a closer look at them, these wisest of every age! Were they all of them perhaps no longer steady on their legs? belated? tottery? *décadents*? [. . .]

[T *The Problem of Socrates* 1]

201

What alone can *our* teaching be?—That no one *gives* a human being his qualities: not God, not society, not his parents or ancestors, not *he himself* [. . .]. *No one* is accountable for existing at all, or for being constituted as he is, or for living in the circumstance and surroundings in which he lives. The fatality of his nature cannot be disentangled from the fatality of all that which has been and will be. He is *not* the result of a special design, a will, a purpose; he is *not* the subject of an attempt to attain to an 'ideal of man' or an 'ideal of happiness' or an 'ideal of morality'—it is absurd to want to *hand over* his nature to some purpose or other. *We* invented the concept 'purpose': in reality purpose is *lacking*. . . . One is necessary, one is a piece of fate, one belongs to the whole, one *is* in the whole—there exists nothing which could judge, measure, compare, condemn our being, for that would be to judge, measure, compare, condemn the whole. . . . *But nothing exists apart from the whole!* —That no one is any longer made accountable, that the kind of being manifested cannot be traced back to a *causa prima*, that the world is a unity neither as sensorium nor as 'spirit', *this alone is the great liberation*—thus alone is the *innocence* of becoming restored. . . . The concept 'God' has hitherto been the greatest *objection* to existence. . . . We deny God; in denying God, we deny accountability: only by doing *that* do we redeem the world.—

[T *Four Great Errors* 8]

202

[. . .] pagans are all who say Yes to life, to whom 'God' is the word for the great Yes to all things [. . .]

[A 55]

203

[. . .] My formula for greatness in a human being is *amor fati*: that one wants nothing to be other than it is, not in the future, not in the past, not in all eternity. Not merely to endure that which happens of necessity, still less to dissemble it—all idealism is untruthfulness in the face of necessity—but to *love* it . . .

[EH *Why I Am So Clever* 10]

204

[. . .] By recognizing Socrates as a *décadent* I [. . .] offered a quite unambiguous proof of how little the certainty of my psychological grasp stood in danger of influence from any kind of moral idiosyncrasy—morality itself as a symptom of *décadence* is a novelty, a unique event of the first order in the history of knowledge. How high above and far beyond the pitiable shallow-pated chatter about optimism *contra* pessimism I had leapt with these conceptions!—I was the first to see the real antithesis

—the *degenerated* instinct which turns against life with subterranean revengefulness [. . .] and a formula of *supreme affirmation* born out of fullness, of superfluity, an affirmation without reservation even of suffering, even of guilt, even of all that is strange and questionable in existence. . . This ultimate, joyfullest, boundlessly exuberant Yes to life is not only the highest insight, it is also the *profoundest*, the insight most strictly confirmed and maintained by truth and knowledge. [. . .]

[EH *The Birth of Tragedy* 2]

Dionysus

205

[. . .] Goethe conceived of a strong, highly cultured human being, skilled in all physical accomplishments, who, keeping himself in check and having reverence for himself, dares to allow himself the whole compass and wealth of naturalness, who is strong enough for this freedom; a man of tolerance, not out of weakness, but out of strength, because he knows how to employ to his advantage what would destroy an average nature; a man to whom nothing is forbidden, except it be *weakness*, whether that *weakness* be called vice or virtue. . . . A spirit thus *emancipated* stands in the midst of the universe with a joyful and trusting fatalism, in the *faith* that only what is separate and individual may be rejected, that in the totality everything is redeemed and affirmed—*he no longer denies*. . . . But such a faith is the highest of all possible faiths: I have baptized it with the name *Dionysos*.—

[T *Expeditions of an Untimely Man* 49]

206

[. . .] For it is only in the Dionysian mysteries, in the psychology of the Dionysian condition, that the *fundamental fact* of the Hellenic instinct expresses itself—its 'will to life'. *What* did the Hellene guarantee to himself with these mysteries? *Eternal* life, the eternal recurrence of life; the future promised and consecrated in the past; the triumphant Yes to life beyond death and change; *true* life as collective continuation of life through procreation, through the mysteries of sexuality. It was for this reason that the *sexual* symbol was to the Greeks the symbol venerable as such, the intrinsic profound meaning of all antique piety. Every individual detail in the act of procreation, pregnancy, birth, awoke the most exalted and solemn feelings. In the teachings of the mysteries, *pain* is sanctified: the 'pains of childbirth' sanctify pain in general—all becoming and growing, all that guarantees the future, *postulates* pain . . . . For the eternal joy in creating to exist, for the will to life eternally to affirm itself, the 'torment of childbirth' *must* also exist eternally. . . . All this is contained in the word Dionysos [. . .] The profoundest instinct of life, the instinct for the future of life, for the eternity of life, is in this word experienced religiously—the actual road to life, procreation, as the *sacred road*. . . . It was only Christianity, with *ressentiment against* life in its foundations, which made of sexuality something impure: it threw *filth* on the beginning, on the prerequisite of our life . . .

[T *What I Owe to the Ancients* 4]

207

The psychology of the orgy as an overflowing feeling of life and energy within which even pain acts as a stimulus provided me with the key to the concept of the *tragic* feeling [. . .]. Affirmation of life even in its strangest and sternest problems, the will to life rejoicing in its own inexhaustibility through the *sacrifice* of its highest types—*that* is what I called Dionysian, *that* is what I recognized as the bridge to the psychology of the *tragic* poet. *Not* so as to get rid of pity and terror, not so as to purify oneself of a dangerous emotion through its vehement discharge—it was thus Aristotle understood it—: but, beyond pity and terror, *to realize in oneself* the eternal joy of becoming—that joy which also encompasses *joy in destruction*. . . . [. . .]—I, the last disciple of the philosopher Dionysos—I, the teacher of the eternal recurrence . . .

[T *What I Owe to the Ancients* 5]

208

[. . .] Affirmation of transitoriness *and destruction*, the decisive element in a Dionysian philosophy, affirmation of antithesis and war, *becoming* with a radical rejection even of the concept '*being*' [. . .]

[EH *The Birth of Tragedy* 3]

209

—Have I been understood?—*Dionysus against the Crucified* . . .

[EH *Why I Am A Destiny* 9]

The Spiritual Body

210

[. . .] It was the sick and dying who despised the body and the earth and invented the things of heaven and the redeeming drops of blood: but even these sweet and dismal poisons they took from the body and the earth!

They wanted to escape from their misery and the stars were too far for them. Then they sighed: 'Oh if only there were heavenly paths by which to creep into another existence and into happiness!' [. . .]

Now they thought themselves transported from their bodies and from this earth, these ingrates. Yet to what do they owe the convulsion and joy of their transport? To their bodies and to this earth. [. . .]

Listen rather, my brothers, to the voice of the healthy body: this is a purer voice and a more honest one.

Purer and more honest of speech is the healthy body, perfect and square-built: and it speaks of the meaning of the earth.

[Z I *Of the Afterworldsmen*]

211

I wish to speak to the despisers of the body. [. . .]

'I am body and soul'—so speaks the child. [. . .]

But the awakened, the enlightened man says: I am body entirely, and nothing beside; and soul is only a word for something in the body. [. . .]

Your little intelligence, my brother, which you call 'spirit', is also an instrument of your body, a little instrument and toy of your great intelligence.

You say 'I' and you are proud of this word. But greater than this—although you will not believe in it—is your body and its great intelligence, which does not say 'I' but performs 'I'. [. . .]

Your Self wants to perish, and that is why you have become despisers of the body! For no longer are you able to create beyond yourselves.

And therefore you are now angry with life and with the earth. An unconscious envy lies in the sidelong glance of your contempt.

I do not go your way, you despisers of the body!
You are not bridges to the Superman!

[Z I *Of the Despisers of the Body*]

212

[. . .] Sensual pleasure: to the rabble the slow fire over
which they are roasted; [. . .] the ever-ready stewing oven
of lust.

Sensual pleasure: innocent and free to free hearts,
the earth's garden-joy, an overflowing of thanks to the
present from all the future.

Sensual pleasure: a sweet poison only to the with-
ered, but to the lion-willed the great restorative and rev-
erently preserved wine of wines. [. . .]

[Z III *Of the Three Evil Things* 2]

213

Has it been observed to what extent a genuine religious
life (both for its favourite labour of microscopic self-
examination and that gentle composure which calls itself
'prayer' and which is a constant readiness for the 'coming
of God'—) requires external leisure or semi-leisure, [. . .]
which is not altogether unfamiliar with the aristocratic
idea that work *degrades*—that is to say, makes soul and
body common? And that consequently modern, noisy,
time-consuming, proud and stupidly proud industriousness educates and prepares precisely for 'unbelief' more
than anything else does?

[BGE 58]

214

[. . .] man's "sinfulness" is not a fact, but merely the interpretation of a fact, namely of physiological depression—
[. . .] When someone cannot get over a "psychological

pain," that is *not* the fault of his "psyche" but, to speak
crudely, more probably even that of his belly [. . .] A
strong and well-constituted man digests his experiences
(his deeds and misdeeds included) as he digests his
meals, even when he has to swallow some tough
morsels. If he cannot get over an experience and have
done with it, this kind of indigestion is as much physiological as is the other—and often in fact merely a consequence of the other.—With such a conception one can,
between ourselves, still be the sternest opponent of all
materialism.—

[GM 3.16]

215

[. . .] It is decisive for the fortune of nations and of
mankind that one should inaugurate culture in the *right
place*—*not* in the 'soul' (as has been the fateful supersti-
tion of priests and quasi-priests): the right place is the
body, demeanor, diet, physiology: the *rest* follows. . . .
[. . .]

[T *Expeditions of an Untimely Man* 47]

216

[. . .] 'Pure spirit' is pure stupidity: if we deduct the nervous system and the senses, the 'mortal frame', *we mis-
calculate*—that's all! . . .

[A 14]

217

[. . .] The *two* physiological facts upon which [Buddhism]
rests and on which it fixes its eyes are: *firstly* an excessive excitability of sensibility [. . .], *then* an over-intellec-
tuality, a too great preoccupation with concepts and
logical procedures under which the personal instinct has

sustained harm [. . .]. On the basis of these physiological conditions a state of *depression* has arisen: against this depression Buddha takes hygienic measures. He opposes it with life in the open air, the wandering life; with moderation and fastidiousness as regards food; with caution towards all alcoholic spirits; likewise with caution towards all emotions which produce gall, which heat the blood; no anxiety, either for oneself or for others. He demands ideas which produce repose or cheerfulness—he devises means of disaccustoming oneself to others. He understands benevolence, being kind, as health-promoting. *Prayer* is excluded, as is *asceticism*; no categorical imperative, no *compulsion* at all, not even within the monastic community (—one can leave it—). All these would have the effect of increasing that excessive excitability. For this reason too he demands no struggle against those who think differently; his teaching resists nothing *more* than it resists the feeling of revengefulness, of antipathy, of *ressentiment* (—'enmity is not ended by enmity': the moving refrain of the whole of Buddhism . . .) [. . .]

[A 20]

218

[. . .] nothing burns one up quicker than the affects of *ressentiment*. Vexation, morbid susceptibility, incapacity for revenge, the desire, the thirst for revenge, poison-brewing in any sense—for one who is exhausted this is certainly the most disadvantageous kind of reaction: it causes a rapid expenditure of nervous energy, a morbid accretion of excretions, for example of gall into the stomach. [. . .]—This was grasped by that profound physiologist Buddha. His 'religion', which one would do better to call a *system of hygiene* [. . .] makes its effect dependent on victory over *ressentiment*: to free the soul of *that*—first step to recovery. 'Not by enmity is enmity ended, by friendship is enmity ended': this stands at the beginning of Buddha's teaching—it is *not* morality that speaks thus, it is physiology that speaks thus.

[EH *Why I Am So Wise* 6]

219

—I shall be asked why I have really narrated all these little things which according to the traditional judgement are matters of indifference [. . .]. Answer: these little things—nutriment, place, climate, recreation, the whole casuistry of selfishness—are beyond all conception of greater importance than anything that has been considered of importance hitherto. It is precisely here that one has to begin to *learn anew*. [. . .]

[EH *Why I Am So Clever* 10]

220

[. . .] And so as to leave no doubt as to my opinion [. . .] I would like to impart one more clause of my moral code against *vice*: [. . .] The clause reads: 'The preaching of chastity is a public incitement to anti-nature. Every expression of contempt for the sexual life, every befouling of it through the concept "impure", is *the* crime against life—is the intrinsic sin against the holy spirit of life.'

[EH *Why I Write Such Good Books* 5]

The Spirit of the Earth

221

[. . .] The Superman is the meaning of the earth. Let your will say: The Superman *shall be* the meaning of the earth!

I entreat you, my brothers, *remain true to the earth*, and do not believe those who speak to you of superterrestrial hopes! They are poisoners, whether they know it or not.

They are despisers of life, atrophying and self-poisoned men, of whom the earth is weary: so let them be gone!

Once blasphemy against God was the greatest blasphemy, but God died, and thereupon these blasphemers died too. To blaspheme the earth is now the most dreadful offence, and to esteem the bowels of the Inscrutable more highly than the meaning of the earth. [. . .]

[Z I *Prologue* 3]

222

[. . .] My Ego taught me a new pride, I teach it to men: No longer to bury the head in the sand of heavenly things, but to carry it freely, an earthly head which creates meaning for the earth! [. . .]

[Z I *Of the Afterworldsmen*]

223

[. . .] Truly, too early died that Hebrew whom the preachers of slow death honour: and that he died too early has since been a fatality for many. [. . .]

Had he only remained in the desert and far from the good and just! Perhaps he would have learned to live and learned to love the earth—and laughter as well!

Believe it, my brothers! He died too early; he himself

would have recanted his teaching had he lived to my age! He was noble enough to recant!

But he was still immature. The youth loves immaturely and immaturely too he hates man and the earth. His heart and the wings of his spirit are still bound and heavy.

But there is more child in the man than in the youth, and less melancholy: he has a better understanding of life and death. [. . .]

[Z I *Of Voluntary Death*]

224

[. . .] Stay loyal to the earth, my brothers, with the power of your virtue! May your bestowing love and your knowledge serve towards the meaning of the earth! Thus I beg and entreat you.

Do not let it fly away from the things of earth and beat with its wings against the eternal walls! Alas, there has always been much virtue that has flown away!

Lead, as I do, the flown-away virtue back to earth—yes, back to body and life: that it may give the earth its meaning, a human meaning!

A hundred times hitherto has spirit as well as virtue flown away and blundered. Alas, all this illusion and blundering still dwells in our bodies: it has there become body and will. [. . .]

May your spirit and your virtue serve the meaning of the earth, my brothers: and may the value of all things be fixed anew by you. To that end you should be fighters! To that end you should be creators! [. . .]

There are a thousand paths that have never yet been trodden, a thousand forms of health and hidden islands of life. Man and man's earth are still unexhausted and undiscovered. [. . .]

You solitaries of today, you who have seceded from society, you shall one day be a people: from you, who have chosen out yourselves, shall a chosen people spring—and from this chosen people, the Superman.

Truly, the earth shall yet become a house of healing! And already a new odour floats about it, an odour that brings health—and a new hope!

[Z I *Of the Bestowing Virtue* 2]

225

[. . .] 'All days shall be holy to me'—thus the wisdom of my youth once spoke: truly, the speech of a joyful wisdom! [. . .]

[Z II *The Funeral Song*]

226

[. . .] 'To be sure: except you become as little children you shall not enter into *this* kingdom of heaven.' (And Zarathustra pointed upwards with his hands.)

'But we certainly do not want to enter into the kingdom of heaven: we have become men, *so we want the kingdom of earth*.'

[Z IV *The Ass Festival* 2]

227

To love men *for the sake of God*—that has been the noblest and most remote feeling attained to among men up till now. That love of man without some sanctifying ulterior objective is one piece of stupidity and animality *more*, that the inclination to this love of man has first to receive its measure, its refinement, its grain of salt and drop of amber from a higher inclination—whatever man it was who first felt and 'experienced' this, however much his tongue may have faltered as it sought to

express such a delicate thought, let him be holy and ven-
erated to us for all time as the man who has soared the
highest and gone most beautifully astray!

[BGE 60]

Despair's Defeat

228

[. . .] All at once I was standing between wild cliffs,
alone, desolate in the most desolate moonlight.

But there a man was lying! And there! The dog,
leaping, bristling, whining; then it saw me coming—then
it howled again, then it *cried out*—had I ever heard a
dog cry so for help?

And truly, I had never seen the like of what I then
saw. I saw a young shepherd writhing, choking, convulsed, his face distorted; and a heavy, black snake was
hanging out of his mouth.

Had I ever seen so much disgust and pallid horror
on a face? Had he, perhaps, been asleep? Then the snake
had crawled into his throat—and there it had bitten itself
fast.

My hands tugged and tugged at the snake—in vain!
they could not tug the snake out of the shepherd's throat.
Then a voice cried from me: 'Bite! Bite!

'Its head off! Bite!'—thus a voice cried from me, my
horror, my hate, my disgust, my pity, all my good and
evil cried out of me with a single cry.

You bold men around me! [. . .]

Solve for me the riddle that I saw, interpret to me
the vision of the most solitary man!

For it was a vision and a premonition: *what* did I see
in allegory? And *who* is it that must come one day?

Who is the shepherd into whose mouth the snake thus crawled? *Who* is the man into whose throat all that is heaviest, blackest will thus crawl?

The shepherd, however, bit as my cry had advised him; he bit with a good bite! He spat far away the snake's head—and sprang up.

No longer a shepherd, no longer a man—a transformed being, surrounded with light, *laughing*! Never yet on earth had any man laughed as he laughed!

O my brothers, I heard a laughter that was no human laughter—and now a thirst consumes me, a longing that is never stilled.

My longing for this laughter consumes me: oh how do I endure still to live! And how could I endure to die now!

[Z III *Of the Vision and the Riddle* 2]

Afterword:
Nietzsche or
the Buddha?

The question might seem strange at first, but it sheds a shaft of light on our postmodern predicament and provides an avenue for a fresh, albeit brief, assessment of Nietzsche.

This book belongs to a series that repositions the great philosophers toward the central questions of life: What is reality? What am I? What are the limiting conditions of my life, and conversely, what are my highest possibilities? Knowing that I must someday die, what must I do to live?

What help is Nietzsche with these questions? It depends to some extent on the degree to which religious faith remains for one a live option. To those who can still believe in an infinitely good, loving, and all-powerful God, a Creator and Parent who cares for our salvation and requires from us only an act of faith before restoring us to the eternal glory of his presence, Nietzsche might well be of no help at all. So long as faith abides, such persons already possess, at least potentially, all the answers they need.

But to those whose God-given instincts for truth have led them to a place where the gift of faith has been inexplicably rescinded, where conscience forbids such faith, and where all theism is placed in doubt—in short, for those who find themselves in a distinctly postmodern condition—Nietzsche becomes more than a help. He becomes a spiritual friend, a great-souled shipmate on uneasy seas. His quest for truth provides bearings for our own, and his plunge into the great questions of life ensures that ours will run sufficiently deep.

Nietzsche looked with suspicion upon spiritual teachings of a traditional sort but was in spite of himself an embodiment of the archetype of the religious prophet and the philosophical seer—not only because of what he said, but also because of the form in which he said it. Nietzsche's teaching has a familiar soteriological structure. First, he diagnoses a fallen state: human beings in their normal, untransformed situation are in a radically unsatisfactory condition. They live diminished, benighted lives, embracing illusions as truth. Second, he provides a prescription for salvation: human beings have within themselves the potential for self-transformation, for conversion to a limitlessly better condition, a fulfilled, enlightened life. Every teaching that presupposes such redemptive possibilities must also entail, as Nietzsche's teaching does, destructive and constructive tasks: first, errors must be destroyed, ignorant modes of living must be abandoned; second, new ways of life in accord with the new aim must be envisioned and adopted.

According to many wisdom traditions, one of the first and most pernicious errors to be thus destroyed is that of false self-assessment: we overestimate what we are and as a result we fail to properly gauge what we can become. Feeling ourselves to be already free and finished, we overlook our poverty, believing instead that we already possess something of the fullness of our human potentiality. Wisdom teachings therefore always involve a war against the complacency of the untrans- formed self. They bombard it with messages of its condi- tionedness, its ignorance, its unfreedom. On this score Nietzsche perfectly fits the traditional mold and his destructive arsenal is as potent as they come. He torpe- does the self's pretension to freedom, proclaiming instead that the self is radically unfree, indeed, that it is a play of impersonal forces. By levelling the metaphysical and moral idols to which humanity clings for identity and meaning, he forces the self to confront its fundamental sense of lack and its strategies for overcoming it.

Yet destruction is never an end in itself. Traditional wisdom teachings, while deconstructing the old self, also provide blueprints for a new form of being. Nietzsche knew instinctively that he had to do the same. Already in the early 1880s he has grown tired of his negations. His alter-ego, Zarathustra, proclaims:

> Free from what? Zarathustra does not care about that! But [. . .] free for what?[1]

In attempting to answer the question "free *for* what?" Nietzsche tries to provide a creative alternative to the nihilist trend of his deconstructive analyses. The question is: does he succeed? Does he provide a viable plan for a new form of life? Does his redemptive vision make good his promise to "bring glad tidings such as there have never been"?[2]

The answer can only be no.

Nietzsche leaves no doubt about the core of *his* gospel: "Once you said 'God' when you gazed upon dis- tant seas; but now I have taught you to say 'Superman'."

The viability of his positive vision therefore depends on the viability of the Superman ideal. Let us ponder the latter by comparing it to another ideal of transformed humanity as it is found in a thinker who held no little fascination for Nietzsche, namely, the Buddha. The comparison is warranted by the fact that the Buddha and Nietzsche are united in their unusual attempt to offer teachings on the psycho-spiritual refinement of the human person *without recourse to theism*.[3] Indeed, we can almost hear the Buddha paraphrasing Nietzsche to his ancient Hindu audience: "Once you said 'God' when you gazed upon distant seas; but now I have taught you to say 'the awakened being'."

The first thing to notice is that the most noble and least problematic aspects of the Superman ideal have already been precisely anticipated by the ideal of the awakened being. In both cases emphasis is laid on a person whose spiritual task is disciplined self-mastery and who therefore, to use Nietzsche's phrase, "no longer flows out into a god." Both ideals envision a person with a lifelong enrollment in the school of self-overcoming. Both cherish inner freedom as a high aim. Both bespeak contemplative types who, contrary to appearances, are not fleeing reality but penetrating into it, habituating their vision to a new repose and teaching it to see the true nature of what lies before it.[4] Both ideals recommend a psycho-physical training that aims at deconditioning the self, freeing it from automatic reactivity, draining from it the poisons of enmity and *ressentiment*, and providing it with access to life's free flow of quality and the concomitant blessings of freedom, plenitude and gratitude.

The second thing to notice is that the most onerous and most problematic aspects of Nietzsche's Superman ideal appear absent from the ideal of the awakened being. We are referring to the Superman's conviction that he is one of the few worthy rather than one of the many worthless human beings, and to the unrepentant selfishness and repudiation of pity that such a stance not only sanctions but recommends. We are, in short, referring to those aspects of the Superman ideal that within thirty years of Nietzsche's death showed themselves liable to heinous misappropriation by ruthless Nazi politicians and demented bigots. By contrast, the Buddhist ideal has over a period of 2500 years been refractory to such abuse, largely because of the moral framework in which it is articulated and from which it refuses to be severed. The person on the path of awakening is taught from the start to see herself as a strand in an interdependent web of being in which the border between "self" and "other" is provisional and ultimately unreal. Recognition of the pure gratuitousness of one's evolutionary grade encourages humility and, most centrally, compassion. Buddhism insists that becoming awake is not only a cognitive matter but a moral-emotive one as well, requiring wisdom and fellow-feeling in equal measure. Perhaps Nietzsche's Superman and the Buddha's awakened being are never so far apart as on this point.

Thirdly, we might briefly notice that the Buddhist ideal has for over two millennia provided a pattern in relation to which countless human beings have shaped their lives. The eminent viability of *its* middle way between God and nothingness[5] has been demonstrated on the testing ground of history. The Superman-ideal, merely a century old, has not yet had a proper historical trial. Some perhaps have tried to shape their lives according to it but as yet they have left little trace. Its chances of becoming a major force in humanity's cultural evolution seem slim.

Some might object to this whole comparison on the grounds that the Buddhist ideal presupposes something Nietzsche explicitly opposes. Buddhism, the objection runs, is only nominally non-theistic; it smuggles in a God-equivalent with the notion of a moral world order (Dharma and karma). And it is precisely the objective reality of such an order that Nietzsche rejects.

The truth of this matter is elusive. At one point in his writings Nietzsche can be heard criticizing both the Buddha and his own teacher, Schopenhauer, for remaining "under the illusion of morality." Yet in another place Nietzsche contradicts himself, praising Buddhism for standing beyond "the self-deception of moral concepts" and for seeing "beyond good and evil."[6] Actually, Nietzsche's contradiction reflects a subtle truth: Buddhism *is* equivocal on this point. The moral order is sometimes spoken of as co-extensive with the real and at other times as a human construct projected onto the void. Buddhism simply stomachs this theoretical paradox and moves forward, insisting on theory's subordination to practice.

Nietzsche, of course, would like to claim that he avoids this paradox by unequivocally rejecting the objective reality of the moral order. Unfortunately, he finds that he cannot consistently do so without landing in absurdity. In seeing good and evil as human constructs, Nietzsche saw "beyond" them. But life cannot be lived, nor can philosophy which concerns itself with the living of life be written, without making moral assessments left and right—as Nietzsche also saw. In order to avoid the claim that his moral judgements reflected some objective order "out there"—a claim he denounced when made by others—Nietzsche was forced to say that his morality was nothing more than personal taste. But a mind of his caliber must have been painfully aware of the solipsistic dead end into which this train of thought inevitably crashes.

Far from being diametrically opposed on the issue of the ontological basis of human valuing, Nietzsche and the Buddha similarly face a monumental paradox. The difference between them lies in the way they endure it.

Finally, our comparison must finally confront Nietzsche's claims that the Buddhist ideal, in its apparent world-negation, says No to life, whereas his Superman says Yes. We must ask two separate questions about these claims. First, how firm is the Superman's Yes? Second, does the Buddhist ideal really say No?

As to the first question: the Superman, Nietzsche tells us, is one who comprehends that human life is lived in an intractable net of fate, a web of necessity in which nothing can be other than the way it is. Yet, by way of a joyous *affirmation* of this very unfreedom, the Superman wins the only, and yet the supreme freedom that a human being can attain. The Superman understands that there is no exit from the eternal recurrence of life in all its joy and horror, and yet utters a great Yes to it in an expression of profound acceptance and love. But now we must ask whether the Superman's prophet, Nietzsche himself, was capable of this affirmation? Apparently not, as this note written while he was at work on *Zarathustra* seems to indicate: "I do not want life *again*. How did I endure it? Creating. What makes me stand the sight of it? The vision of the overman who *affirms* life. I have tried to affirm it *myself*—alas!"[7] What? Do the Superman and his affirmations exist only in the imagination of a literary man? Nor do we need to overemphasize this little aside. Students of Nietzsche's life and work soon learn of a man whose affirmative moods regularly alternated with others of black despair. The levers needed to redeem the world (as the Superman is thought to do) must surely be made of more than the wisps of changeable moods.

Nietzsche himself seems to have understood this. He saw that in order for the affirmative mood to be more than ephemeral, it would have to discover some wider basis in the body, in a "great health." Consequently, he called for a "physio-psychology", a somatic discipline that could, as it were, carry ideas to the marrow. And yet it is precisely this, his Alpine jaunts notwithstanding, that Nietzsche lacked. When he wishes to underscore the somatic dimension of the Superman's eradication of *ressentiment* Nietzsche finds himself turning to the Buddha:

> [. . .] nothing burns one up quicker than the affects of *ressentiment*. [. . .] This was grasped by that profound physiologist Buddha. His 'religion', which one would do better to call a *system of hygiene* [. . .] makes its effect dependent on victory over *ressentiment*: [. . .] 'Not by enmity is enmity ended, by friendship is enmity ended': this stands at the beginning of Buddha's teaching—it is *not* morality that speaks thus, it is physiology that speaks thus.[8]

Nietzsche would have been interested to know that Zen Buddhists sometimes refer to their training as "attaining in the body."

This takes us to the second question: Is the Buddhist ideal really life-negating? In the century since Nietzsche's death scholars have simply buried this misconception. Concurring in their consensus but unique in the language he has found to express it is the American scholar N.P. Jacobson:

> Buddhism is the first system of orientation and devo-
> tion to affirm that individual men and women . . .
> embody an aim largely hidden from conscious
> thought toward greater fullness of quality in their
> experience.
>
> Buddhist meditation is a discipline that unravels
> the ego-dominated life by reconditioning one's bodi-
> ly-sensitive self and] shifting the center of gravity
> over to the flow of unstructured quality in the pass-
> ing *now* . . . .
>
> . . . For those who are able . . . to maintain
> their center of gravity in the passing *now*, nature
> confers upon them the one sign they have succeed-
> ed. That sign is joy—not pleasure, but joy . . . cele-
> brating the wonder of being everyday alive. . . .
>
> . . . This is what it means to be free, free to cel-
> ebrate the aesthetic richness which comes as a gift
> beyond the claims of the self.[9]

In the summer of 1881, at the age of thirty-six, Nietzsche
wrote to his friend, Peter Gast: "I think of myself as the
scrawl which an unknown power scribbles across a sheet
of paper, to try out a new pen." [10]. It is a moment of
dejection, perhaps, but we can read something else
between the lines: the confession of a genius that he is
but a vehicle through which larger forces shape the
world.

In the end we must admit that Nietzsche himself was
better at destroying than creating, more skillful in
answering the question "free from what?" than "free for
what?" But, as Nietzsche himself has taught us to say: we
are not ungrateful. There is a sense in which Nietzsche
sacrificed his life for us, offered it as an experiment to
test the consequences of sailing on a sea where all Gods

have died. His books, written in the blood of this sacrifice, constitute a school through which everyone who wishes to think deeply about life's enduring questions should pass—but only if they can afford the tuition: the exposure of all cherished convictions to Nietzsche's relentless hammer. And if our above remarks have any validity, Nietzsche has given us at least one other gift. He has made a western clearing for an ancient path of self-transformation now freed of its commitments to premodern Asian cultures.

> Will it perhaps be said of us one day that we too, steering westward hoped to reach an India—but that it was our fate to be wrecked against infinity? Or, my brothers? Or?[11]

---

[1] Z of I *The Way of the Creator.*

[2] EH *Why I Am A Destiny* 1.

[3] During its long Asian pilgrimage Buddhism often took on theistic forms but we are not concerned with these here. It might also be mentioned that the teachings of the Buddha and Nietzsche share a number of other basic points of contact: the unsubstantiality of the "I", a preference for the key of becoming rather than the key of being; a strategic subordination of logic to psychology; a view of the world-process as a quenchless thirst (will to power, *raga, tanha*). Nietzsche always believed, however, that the cardinal difference between his teaching and the Buddha's was that the latter's was life-negating. I address this misperception below.

[4] GM 2:24; T *What the Germans Lack* 6.

[5] Nietzsche describes the Superman as a "victor over both God and nothingness." GM 2.24.

[6] A 20.

7 Kaufmann, trans., *The Gay Science*, 19.

8 EH *Why I Am So Wise* 6.

9 Nolan   Pliny   Jacobson,   *Understanding   Buddhism*, Carbondale, Southern Illinois University Press, 1986, 38, 63, 86–8.

10 Stern, *Friedrich Nietzsche*, 38.

11 D 575.

Index